Practical Genealogy

BRIAN SHEFFEY

Practical Genealogy

50 Simple Steps to Research Your Diverse Family History

ROCKRIDGE
PRESS

For general information on our other products and services or to obtain technical support, please contact our Customer Care Department within the United States at (866) 744-2665, or outside the United States at (510) 253-0500.

Rockridge Press publishes its books in a variety of electronic and print formats. Some content that appears in print may not be available in electronic books, and vice versa.

Interior and Cover Designer: John Calmeyer
Art Producer: Tom Hood
Editor: Andrea Leptinsky
Production Editor: Nora Milman

Illustration © Bakani/Creative Market, cover; Lake Erie Maps and Prints/Alamy, p. 26; Historic Collection/Alamy, p. 54; ART Collection/Alamy, p. 58; Andrew Fare/Alamy, p. 70; Shutterstock/LiliGraphie, p. 78; Shutterstock.I Pilon, p. 84; Aviation History Collection/Alamy, p. 98; Photograph © iStock/Gisele, p. 40; Shutterstock/PSV, p. 40; Archive Pics/Alamy, p. 100; Alamy, p. 110; World History Archive/Alamy, p. 114; courtesy Library of Congress, p. 122; Wim Wiskerke/Alamy, p. 143; courtesy of Tropenmuseum, part of the National Museum of World Cultures, p.144; courtesy Lewis Hine, p. 144; Trevor Chriss/Alamy, p. 150; Author photo courtesy of Alexis Yeldell-Williams.

ISBN: Print 978-1-64611-566-2 | eBook 978-1-64611-567-9

Ro

In loving memory of my parents,

Joseph C. Sheffey, Jr., and

Barbara A. Turner Sheffey

CONTENTS

COMPREHEND HOW TO ACTIVITY REFLECT HEADS UP

INTRODUCTION

My foray into genealogy began in 2007 when I pondered what to give my then 72-year-old father for his birthday. Discovering and sharing his family's American origin story seemed to be the perfect gift. It was. It took less than a day for the research to hook me, and the journey I've undertaken since then has been profound.

I was an American living abroad in England when I began my ancestral journey. For the first time in my life, I felt like an American. Genealogy gave me an American identity that I never had while growing up.

My genealogy adventures unveiled an unexpectedly rich and diverse connection to the formation of America. I am the child of European royalty, America's founding fathers, and Native Americans, as well as free and enslaved Africans. My ancestors were among the first to settle the British colonies of Connecticut, Massachusetts, Pennsylvania, Rhode Island, Virginia, the Carolina territory, New Sweden, and New Amsterdam. My early colonial-era Native, European, and African ancestry—plus my early-twentieth-century Jewish ancestry—is the foundational story of the United States. In truth, genealogy has taught me more about American history and the American experience than any class I have ever taken.

My passion for genealogy led me to create the research website Genealogy Adventures in 2010, followed by a podcast series that began in 2016. Through these platforms, I've been able to share strategies, approaches, and resources for researching poorly documented ancestors.

My expertise is in mid-Atlantic and Southern research and genetic genealogy, with an emphasis on the intersection of white, black, and Native American genealogy. I have used this knowledge to solve seemingly impossible cases of unknown parentage from colonial America to the present using DNA and paper trail evidence. Through every bit of research, I've always been driven by the belief that genealogy is an opportunity to connect with people from different backgrounds, both at home and around the globe.

I do have some words of caution for you before you begin your research, however. We never know what stories our genealogical research will unveil. Before you begin, give some thought to how you will process and handle some of the difficult histories you might uncover.

From enslaved Africans to indentured and imprisoned Irish and Scottish ancestors, I have faced and overcome brick wall after brick wall in my research. You will face brick walls, too, but they are not insurmountable. In this book, I will share some of the strategies, tactics, and out-of-the-box thinking I have used successfully to overcome common obstacles that you might come across.

Using these approaches, you will discover ancestors who left obscured, hidden, partially erased, or fragmented footsteps in the sands of history.

Welcome to the start of your genealogy adventures.

WHO

WHAT

WHY

WHERE

WHEN

STEP 1

COMPREHEND

The 5 Fundamental Ws of Research

The most important step in genealogical research is the first one. Step 1 is when we answer the 5 fundamental Ws: Who, What, Why, Where, and When. Each "W" needs to be answered for each of the ancestors we research.

> *Information is core to genealogical research. That sounds obvious, but what is not so clear is that we can't take the documents we discover at face value. It is natural to become excited when we discover a record or a story about an ancestor, but that discovery is merely the first stage of the research process. Next, we must analyze the information, using critical-thinking skills.*

Critical thinking allows us to overcome our biases, lack of background knowledge and information—even our own prejudices. It is critical thinking that lets you figure out, for example, if the document you found is for the person you are researching or just someone who happened to share the same name.

Answering the 5 fundamental Ws will help you begin your research using a thorough critical-thinking approach.

Look for Defining Critical Thinking at https://www.criticalthinking.org/pages/defining-critical-thinking/766.

Who

Who seems the most obvious question to start with when analyzing records. The name of our ancestor is one part of the *who* we must answer, but there are two other important considerations: primary informants and secondary informants.

A primary informant is the ancestor we are researching. He or she directly supplied information such as a name, place of birth, and year of birth for documents like marriage certificates, marriage bonds, voter registration records, property transactions and deeds, passports, insurance and mortgage applications, Native American tribal enrollment applications, or bank account applications.

Secondary informants are people other than the ancestor we are researching who supplied details for a document. Birth and death certificates, as well as baptismal and christening records, are perfect examples of documents where a secondary informant provided the information. Was the secondary informant a family member? A local or state official? A doctor, lawyer, teacher, or religious leader? How well could the informant have known the person named in the record? We must always be aware that secondary informants may not have supplied the correct information.

What

What was the purpose of the record? If your ancestor wanted to serve—or, alternatively, avoid serving—in World War I, for example, he could have misled the draft board about his age to either join or avoid enlisting in the military. Were your ancestors too young to marry? One or both marriage partners may have provided an incorrect year of birth, making them appear old enough to be legally married. This happened more often than you might think.

Always remember that people supply information for documents to achieve a specific end. If the parents' names and the ancestor's location are correct on a document, don't be thrown from the trail by an incorrect year of birth.

Why

Why is all about motivation. Our ancestors' lives were influenced by external events and factors. They may have moved from one place to another for a variety of reasons: land that was no longer fertile or had become more expensive, bankruptcies, debt, or even a desire for a fresh start. Understanding the specific external factors that may have impacted an ancestor's life can guide you to helpful information sources such as history books and land records. If your ancestor had to move because his land was no longer fruitful, what new territories opened up in that time period where he could have moved? Where were other people from his community moving to for new farmland?

Native Americans moved or were removed by force as a result of warfare and skirmishes with colonists during the colonial period or were forcibly relocated by the federal government after the colonies became a republic. Enslaved African Americans often found themselves in new places after being sold away or bequeathed to a member of an enslaver's family and taken away when that family member moved. Free African Americans, particularly in Virginia, moved to the West and the South as Virginia's

Black Code, which limited their freedoms, became increasingly oppressive.

Why also addresses discrepancies in different documents. Why was an ancestor named as Gideon in one document and Gibson in another? Some inconsistencies like this are due to human error. It could be that the clerk who filled in the marriage certificate details heard the name "Gibson" instead of "Gideon." If your ancestor Gibson couldn't read or write, he would have never known a mistake was made on his marriage certificate. Or, in transcribing a very old record, the transcriber may have misread old-fashioned cursive writing.

Where

Locations are important. If two documents provide different places for an ancestor's birth, you must ask yourself why. Did the parish, county, or state boundaries change during that person's life? Getting to the bottom of such discrepancies will require additional historical research.

> *Language might be an explanation for discrepancies or inaccurate information if your ancestor was an immigrant with little to no understanding of English. Perhaps he or she did not understand the question and provided an answer related to something else entirely.*

If the document trail ends suddenly and your ancestor seemingly disappeared from the face of the earth, *where* can also help you track down where they ended up. Researching the movements of immediate and extended family is key. For instance, could the ancestor have moved to be near family members?

> *Look for "William Holloway, Martha Branson, and Phebe Crispin: A Genealogical Game of Hide and Seek" at https://genealogyadventures.net/5Ws.*

When

Was the document you found created at the time of a life event, as in a marriage certificate? Or was the information provided by a secondary informant relying on memory, as with a death certificate? In some documents, such as a family bible, certain entries may have been written at the time of an event, like a birth or a death, or years after the event in question. Always remember that memories can be faulty.

> *Chronological order is also an essential aspect of* when. *You may have the names of an ancestor's parents but not their years of birth. If you find a record for someone showing they were born before their parents were born, you obviously do not have the correct document! This point may sound obvious and even silly, but it is important to keep in mind nonetheless.*

If a record indicates a female ancestor started to have children when she was under the age of 15, this should raise a red flag. Although girls did have children at 13 or 14 in the colonial period, it was not commonplace. You will need to make an extra effort to find the documents proving the year your female ancestor was born, at the very least, along with the year she was married. Compare her age or date of birth on these records to the birth record you have found to determine which is more reliable.

Activity

Think about a descendant or future family member researching your life and the lives of your parents and grandparents. With that in mind, answer these questions on a sheet of paper:

- Has your name consistently appeared the same way in every official document (e.g., driver's license, job applications, census forms, phone book)? If not, list the some of the documents in which it appears differently.
- Have you always used your full name?
  - Do you sometimes use your full middle name and at other times use your middle initial?
  - Have you ever used a nickname or a shortened version of your name (e.g., Bill or Will instead of William? Betsy or Liz instead of Elizabeth?)?
- Have you ever moved? What was the reason behind those moves?
  - University or vocational training?
  - Job opportunities or career advancement?
  - Military service?
  - Marriage or divorce?
- Has the year or date of your birth appeared consistently in all official documents? If not, list the documents in which it appears differently.

If you have thought of any discrepancies, note why these occurred. What clues are there that these records and documents refer to you and not to someone else with the same name?

For women, think about how your name has changed (or may change in the future) through marriage or divorce, and how easy or difficult it might be for a descendant or future family member to find the correct records for you as your last name changes over time.

Repeat this exercise for your parents and your grandparents, if you are at a stage in your research that enables you to do so.

Now that you have explored the 5 Ws, it's time for you to start thinking about where to begin your own research! Keep the 5 Ws in mind and apply them as you work your way through the remaining steps.

STEP 2

What's Your Starting Point?

At its heart, genealogy is a problem-solving process. As with any process, you'll need a clearly defined strategy to be successful. Your strategy should consist of a series of steps, each addressing a specific goal.

It is tempting to dive in, skip a few steps, and go back as many generations as you can. That would be a mistake. Genealogy isn't about speed—it's about endurance. Keep it simple to start with. Don't frustrate yourself by setting overly ambitious goals. Just start at the beginning.

In addition to becoming frustrated or overwhelmed, by going full steam ahead you are likely to:

- Miss essential records you need to find for your ancestors.
- Miss important information in the records you find in your research.
- Not spend the necessary time familiarizing yourself with the vast range of documents available both online and in libraries, repositories, and specialist collections.
- Not develop an effective research strategy.
- Not be able to meet the genealogically accepted standards of proof, including failing to correctly add sources and citations for the records you have included as proof for an ancestor.

Getting Started

There are two things to consider before you begin your research: a research goal and research questions.

A research goal is focused on a specific research task; research questions support you in meeting your goal. For example, if your goal is documenting the marriage of your grandparents, then your questions could be: When and where were your grandparents married, and who married them? Where can you find a copy of their marriage license and marriage certificate?

Starting a FAN Club

In genealogy, we refer to Friends, Associates, and Neighbors as a FAN club. FAN clubs can provide invaluable information. It is good practice to politely ask the FAN club person you are speaking to how they know the information they have provided. Did they witness the event firsthand? Are they repeating a rumor they heard? Was this information that a third party told them, and if so, what was the name of the third party? (Be mindful, however, that the person you are speaking with may not reveal their source due to privacy reasons.)

Research questions need to be focused and specific, and they should incorporate the 5 Ws. Pick one question to start with. As you gather the answers to this question, assess its effectiveness. You can always revise it if you are not achieving the results you need.

Getting into the groove of a new research process doesn't have to be daunting. The process that lays the foundation for achieving genealogical research success could look like this:

1 Identify your first goal. It should be a task you can accomplish within a reasonable amount of time.

2 Create small, manageable steps to achieve your first goal. Write down each step. Do the same for the rest of your goals.

- For example, your first goal might be finding basic information about your mother's father (your maternal grandfather). Your first step could be interviewing your mother for information about her father's date and place of birth, where he went to school, what his occupation was, where he worked, and where he lived throughout his life.
- Your second step could be interviewing your mother's siblings about your grandfather, asking them the same questions you asked your mother.
- A third step might be finding pictures of your maternal grandfather.
- Further steps could include finding his school report cards, religious ceremony records, and military service records as well as any newspaper articles that mentioned him. Throughout these steps, you will be collecting as much information about your grandfather as you can—basically, answering each of the 5 Ws.

3 Your second goal could be repeating the same exercise for your mother's mother (your maternal grandmother).

4 Your third goal could be repeating the same exercise for your maternal grandfather's siblings. Your next goal could be finding the same information about your maternal grandmother's siblings, and so on.

Minimum Family Information

When conducting your research, remember that the absolute minimum information you need for each ancestor is the person's:

- Full name
- Birth date and location
- Marriage date and location
- Death date and location

You will also need the full names, birth dates, and death dates for all siblings.

Standard genealogical practice is to use the following format for recording dates: DD MMM YYYY (e.g., 27 Jan 2019).

Take this time to familiarize yourself with the staggering array of documents you can find or access for your ancestors. Explore all the information each document contains and how this information can answer your 5 Ws as well as raise additional questions to answer.

Be aware that your goals will change as you grow more experienced as a researcher.

Start a Research Log

Save the information you are gathering in a research log. Use a format that works best for you, such as a Microsoft Word document, a Microsoft Excel spreadsheet, or an OpenOffice Writer document. If you prefer a non-digital option, you may decide to use a binder or folder to organize your research.

Your log should include:

- Your research goals and supporting research questions, along with the steps needed to achieve your goals.
- What you already know, such as what you have learned from your family interviews.
- All the research and document sources you may need to find or confirm information that will provide evidence for your research questions.
- Information you find from the sources you are using to document your findings.
- Your research notes and analysis.
- Any additional research questions you develop based on your research.

- Resolution of any information conflicts (e.g., differences in the spelling of someone's name, date of birth, or place of residence) and a conclusion about the discrepancy or what additional research is required to address it.

Keep in mind that the first research document you create is going to be the launching point for your future research. We will explore logs more fully in Step 5: Document Your Research (page 17), Step 6: Develop a Research Outline (page 20), and Step 25: Cite Sources (page 80).

Once you have recorded everything in your research log, you will probably have quite a list of steps to work though. Don't be intimidated! There is a solution that will help you avoid feeling overwhelmed, and it's called organization. In Step 3: Stay Organized (page 10), we will explore how to keep your research organized.

Look for "Research Logs" on the FamilySearch website.

In your research log, remember to write down who provided you with which pieces of information. During your research, you will come to realize—and should always note—that some information sources are more reliable than others.

Name-Hunting Research Tip

When you record names, always use the name as written on a birth certificate. You can include shortened versions of the name your ancestor used, including any nicknames. For female ancestors, this means using their maiden name—the surname they were born with, not their married name.

Involve Your Family

Speaking with immediate and extended family members can help you fill in any gaps in the information you have found. The more information you have at this first stage, the better you will be able to search for additional information in online databases, in your local library, or at your state's archives.

Arrange a time to speak with your parents, grandparents, and great-grandparents, if they are alive. Speak with other older relatives as well, such as uncles and aunts. The older generations in a family can provide a wealth of information, histories, old documents, and photographs.

In the course of reaching out to family members, you may discover that one of them has already done a substantial amount of work documenting your family. Ask them to meet with you to discuss the information they have and how you can use it in your research. Please note that researchers always acknowledge the contributions others have made to advance their research. Passing off someone else's research as your own is a form of plagiarism. On a more positive note, finding the research others have done could save you hours, months, and even years of research.

STEP 3

Stay Organized

Organizing your research is vital to achieving your research goals. This process will keep your documentation, records, and source materials in order. It will also help you keep track of the information you have gathered that answers the 5 Ws in your research process as well as the work that remains to be done to answer those five questions.

In the early stages of your research, jotting down notes on paper and saving them in a binder or notebook is a practical way to organize the basic information you'll be gathering.

As you move on, you may want to switch over to your computer and store your information using a word processor or note-taking program.

Once your research becomes more developed and your organization needs become more complex, you may need to use a more advanced method of organizing your research. I suggest waiting until after you have been researching for a while before deciding on a more detailed organizational approach. By then, you should have a good understanding of how you naturally process and record information.

Look for "Organizing Your Files" on FamilySearch Wiki, which provides guidance on how to develop a research organization strategy that supports the way you research.

A more advanced organizational solution could include software like Ancestral Quest, Family Tree Maker, or Roots Magic. Spend some time researching the organizational platform you are interested in using. Depending on your research style, needs, and personal preferences, some programs will support your research work better than others.

For Example

My research needs grew to require something that I could access anywhere at any time. Organizing this was a daunting task because I have over 150,000 individuals in my family tree. To address this, I created a file directory structure on my computer. You can see how this was organized on the next page.

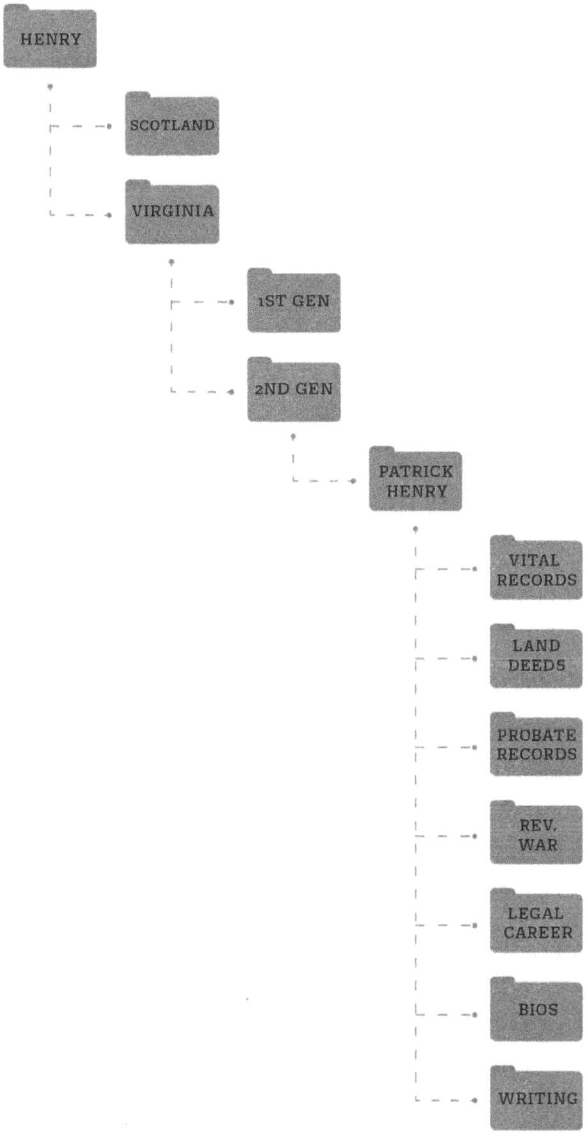

What you see is the main computer directory structure for the Henry family. This is labeled as "Henry," which you will see is the first directory folder. The next level, or subdirectory, is based on the places the Henry family lived: Scotland and Virginia, in this instance. You will see another set of subdirectories based on the different Henry family generations. The first generation of the family in colonial Virginia has its own folder (1st Gen). All the members of the family who were the first generation born in colonial Virginia are kept together within the 1st Gen folder. Family members in the second generation are located in the 2nd Gen folder, and so on, for each subsequent generation of the Henry family.

In this example, you can see that Patrick Henry is part of the second generation of the Henry family born in colonial America. All the materials, documents, resources, information, etc., for Patrick Henry are stored in subfolders within his subdirectory.

This organizational structure supports the way that I work and process information, enabling me to quickly access the large volume of Patrick Henry–related information and records I've collected.

It also allows me to back up my research on external hard drives, memory cards, and cloud storage solutions to ensure it is not lost. We will explore other ways to preserve your research in Step 10: Preserve and Share Your Family's Story (page 36) and Step 12: Save Your Photos (page 41).

Now would be a good time to think about how you process information. Understanding this is important when it comes to navigating genealogical-related databases, which is the subject of Step 4.

STEP 4

Explore Helpful Online Databases

There is a treasure trove of information in online genealogy databases and resources for you to explore. Take the time to familiarize yourself with all the records and sub-databases each of these online services host. You will gain a better understanding of how different genealogical research databases are organized, the key terms they use, the range of records and information that can be found, and how different databases can answer different research questions.

Database	Paid or Free	Description with Link
AfriGeneas	FREE	A website devoted to African American genealogy, genealogical research, and African American resources in general. It is also an active African Ancestry research community. http://www.afrigeneas.com
Ancestry.com	$	A for-profit genealogy company with extensive databases. It also includes an online family tree builder. https://www.ancestry.com

Database	Paid or Free	Description with Link
Archives.gov	FREE	A free online repository with a section dedicated to genealogical research. https://www.archives.gov
The Bureau of Refugees, Freedmen, and Abandoned Lands (the Freedmen's Bureau)	FREE	Index of census returns, registers, and lists of freedmen. The Bureau of Refugees, Freedmen, and Abandoned Lands (often called the Freedmen's Bureau) was created in 1865 at the end of the American Civil War to supervise relief efforts, including education; health care; food and clothing; refugee camps; legalization of marriages; employment; labor contracts; and securing back pay, bounty payments, and pensions. These records include letters and endorsements, sent and received; account books; applications for rations; applications for relief; court records; labor contracts; registers of bounty claimants, complaints, contracts, disbursements, freedmen-issued rations, and patients; reports; rosters of officers and employees; special and general orders and circulars, received and issued; and records relating to claims, court trials, property restoration, and homesteads. https://www.familysearch.org/wiki (Search on the term "African American Freedmen's Bureau Records.")
Chronicling America (from the Library of Congress)	FREE	Free searchable online database of over 2,400 U.S. newspapers. https://chroniclingamerica.loc.gov

Database	Paid or Free	Description with Link
Cyndi's List	FREE	Thousands of genealogical resource links that have been categorized and cross-referenced. https://www.cyndislist.com
Familypedia	FREE	A collaborative family history encyclopedia featuring a genealogy information source and database. https://familypedia.wikia.org
FamilySearch	FREE	A free online genealogy and family history guide developed by the Church of Jesus Christ of Latter-Day Saints that lists websites, provides research strategies, and suggests records and resources to help you find ancestors from all over the world. Also includes an online family tree builder. https://www.familysearch.org
Find a Grave	FREE	An online database with millions of cemetery and burial records. https://www.findagrave.com
Fold3	$	Features collections of original military records and Native American enrollment records. Many of the records come from the U.S. National Archives, the British National Archives, and other international records. https://www.fold3.com

Database	Paid or Free	Description with Link
JewishGen	FREE	JewishGen is a nonprofit organization founded in 1987 as an international electronic resource for Jewish genealogy. https://www.jewishgen.org
Library of Virginia	FREE	The online home for the most comprehensive resource and databases in the world for the study of Virginia history, culture, and government. http://www.lva.virginia.gov
Lowcountry Africana	FREE	A free website sponsored by the Magnolia Plantation Foundation of Charleston, South Carolina, dedicated to African American genealogy and history in South Carolina, Georgia, and Florida. https://lowcountryafricana.com
MyHeritage	$	One of the leading global providers for discovering, preserving, and sharing family history with numerous databases. It is a popular platform for those with Jewish ancestry. https://www.myheritage.com
New England Historic Genealogical Society	FREE	America's oldest genealogical society, providing education and research resources with over 1.4 billion records. https://www.americanancestors.org
Newspapers .com	$	The largest online newspaper archive, consisting of 531 million-plus pages of historical editions of 14,400-plus newspapers from around the United States and beyond. https://www.newspapers.com

Database	Paid or Free	Description with Link
Unknown No Longer (Virginia Museum of History and Culture)	FREE	A database of the names of all the enslaved Virginians that appear in the museum's unpublished documents. https://www.virginiahistory.org/collections/unknown-no-longer-database-virginia-slave-names

Now that you have taken some time to familiarize yourself with some of the popular online databases and spent some time considering how you will initially organize your findings, it's time to think about how you will document the discoveries you make during the course of your research. This includes how you will enter the information you find in your research log.

STEP 5

Document Your Research

You've spent some time determining your starting point and explored how to keep your research organized. Now it's time to think about documenting your research. Part of the documentation process includes citing your research sources, which we will cover in Step 25: Cite Sources (page 80). For now, let's focus on how to document your overall findings.

The Genealogical Proof Standard

How can you feel confident that the conclusions you come to in your genealogical research—which will sometimes lead you to contradictory or unclear evidence—are reasonable and reliable? By measuring your work against the same standard used by serious genealogists. It's called the Genealogical Proof Standard, and it requires that you:

- Always search as widely as possible for sources of information.
- Make sure to cite every source completely and accurately.
- Analyze all evidence and resolve any contradictions.
- Make a reasonable argument for your conclusions.

Look for "The Genealogical Proof Standard" on the FamilySearch Wiki, which gives more information on this topic, including a sample proof argument.

At this stage, you have probably started to collect the names, dates, and places for the first three or four generations of your family and entered them into your research log. You've made notes and saved copies of various records and documents. But can you remember where you found your great-grandfather's birth certificate? Or where you found the record that confirmed your grandparents' marriage date?

Genealogy requires evidence to prove the correct dates of births, marriages, and deaths, as well as correct names and residences. Keeping track of every document, record, and piece of information, as well as where you found them, is a critical part of genealogy.

> *Proper documentation lays the groundwork to support your research strategies and goals. It confirms that the information you have is correct and flags information that still needs to be verified, helping you stay organized and efficient. You will quickly lose the thread of your research if you lump all your documents and records in one place.*

Remember that evidence is required regardless of whether you're relying on a primary informant (an ancestor who directly supplied information, such as a birth certificate) or a secondary informant (someone other than the ancestor who supplied details, such as a regional history book, slave deed of sale, or Native American oral tribal history).

Use Your Research Log

Don't forget to use your research log! It's an excellent tool for organizing and documenting your work. You can do this in real time as you access each record, or you can make notes and document your findings at the end of each research session. Keep in mind that you can easily access hundreds of documents and records in a single research session. Chances are, if you put off documenting your work until some future point in time, you just won't do it. What happens when you fail to document your work? It starts a chain reaction that creates confusion, duplicated searches for information and records, overlooked or missing evidence, and unsubstantiated theories or assertions.

Five Steps to Document Your Research

1. Photocopy all records and source documents that you find in paper form and save all digital images.

2. Identify the source for each record or document. For photocopies, add this information to the front or back of the document. For digital images, include this information in the file name.

3. Create a document filing number for each record or document. For photocopies, add this information to the front or back of the document. For digital images, include this information in the file name.

4 Add the document number to your research log and summarize the events and people you found in the document.

5 Include an assessment of the data's reliability in the footnote comment field of your report.

If you're using a binder for your research log, adding documents like the ones referenced previously will be easy. If you've decided to use a digital format, like a Word document, you can take a picture of the paper documents or pictures that you have collected and add those to your digital research log.

Keep all your research information up-to-date. Don't start more research before updating your research log with the latest information you gathered. This practice will keep you on track toward achieving your research goals and set you up for success when it comes to developing a research outline, a subject we will be exploring in Step 6.

STEP 6

Develop a Research Outline

Creating a research outline will help you organize and structure your work, allowing you to see the overall picture. Your outline should consist of seven steps:

1 Clearly identify your research goals.

2 Draft your research steps.

3 Analyze the information you collect.

4 Evaluate the sources you use.

5 Create a working hypothesis.

6 Reflect and assess on the information you have found.

7 Save your work and update your research log.

Set Research Goals

The best research goals tend to be based on clear research questions. For example:

RESEARCH QUESTION Who were the 45 enslaved children of Moses Williams?

RESEARCH GOAL Find the 45 enslaved children of Moses Williams.

RESEARCH QUESTION Is Daniel Christian the father of Thomas Christian?

RESEARCH GOAL Verify that Daniel Christian is the father of Thomas Christian.

RESEARCH QUESTION Was my maternal great-grandfather Jewish?

RESEARCH GOAL Identify my unknown Jewish maternal great-grandfather.

Take the Right Steps

Breaking your research goals down into small, measurable steps will help you stay organized and keep you from getting overwhelmed. Remember to add the steps to your research log so you can see the progress you've made as well the work that still needs to be completed. Here are some examples of research steps:

- Prove Joe Bloggs's date of birth.
- Verify the marriage date for Joe Bloggs and Jane Doe.
- Confirm the names of all of Joe Bloggs and Jane Doe's children.
- Find the land purchase records and deeds for Joe Bloggs between 1870 and 1890.

Analyze Your Information

Once you've accumulated a significant amount of information, you will need to conduct an analysis. This means examining each individual document to determine whether it is accurate. You'll need to consider general questions, such as whether the material you gathered comes from primary or secondary sources—that is, was the information the result of firsthand experience of an event, or was it hearsay?

You'll also need to delve into questions about the specific information you've uncovered. For example:

- How accurate was all the information on your great-grandmother's marriage certificate? Some information provided may be more reliable than the rest. How does the information compare to similar information in other documents related to her? Is she always found in the same county? Is her year of birth consistent in all the documents you've found?
- Who were the informants who supplied the information? Were they family members? Neighbors? Professionals, such as doctors or lawyers? How reliable were these informants? How much would they have known about the person about whom they supplied information?

Evaluate Your Sources

Did you take your information from an original document, a photocopy, a transcription, or an indexed version of a document? The more removed you are from the original record, the more chances there are for errors to occur. Remember to evaluate both primary and secondary sources of information for accuracy.

Form a Working Hypothesis

A working hypothesis will guide you in your research and also highlight gaps and information discrepancies that require further research. For example, your hypothesis might be that Amos Harlan was the father of Ezekiel Harlan. Your research might show that there are no records proving a biological connection between the two men, but there is a land map showing that an Amos Harland and an Ezekiel Harlan lived next door to one another. Since the map doesn't give you definitive information, you'll need to continue your search. An ideal find would be a will for Amos, citing a son named Ezekiel.

These considerations will result in identifying and noting other research steps you need to include in your research. Adding new or additional steps will mean updating your research log with these new considerations and findings.

Reflect and Assess

At this point, you will need to reflect on everything you've learned about the ancestor you are researching and assess whether or not you have met your research goal. If you haven't been able to satisfy that goal, this is when you will determine what additional steps you need to take to do so.

Save Your Work

Saving your work is the final stage of the process. I suggest saving your work before you end your research for the day. Life happens. You may plan to save your research a day or two afterward and then forget to do so. If you don't save your work every day, you risk not having the necessary information later on when you need to refer to a document you uncovered or the place where you found it.

For an example of a genealogical research article, see Appendix A: Finding a Lost Connection to the Weeping Time Slave Sale (1859, Savannah, Georgia).

Now that you have spent some time exploring some of the basic and fundamental aspects of genealogical research, it's time to reflect on the new concepts you have learned.

CONCRETE EXPERIENCE
doing/having an experience
REFLECTIVE OBSERVATION
reviewing/reflecting on the experience
ABSTRACT CONCEPTUALIZATION
concluding/learning from the experience
ACTIVE EXPERIMENTATION
planning/trying out what you have learned

STEP 7

Reflect

REFLECT

Congratulations on making huge strides in your new genealogical research endeavor! Take some time to reflect on the new skills and information we have covered.

Check in with yourself by answering the following questions:

- How well do you understand the best ways to conduct genealogical research?
- How confident are you in creating your first research log?
- How confident are you in developing a series of steps to reach a research goal?
- Can you recall the difference between a primary information source and a secondary information source?

Give yourself permission to acknowledge if you are still unclear about a topic we have explored together. Reread a previous step, if you need to. Remember, genealogy is an endurance activity, not a sprint.

Make sure you really understand and can apply the fundamental introductory concepts you have explored up to this point. You will need to understand them before we move on to the more complex aspects of genealogy research.

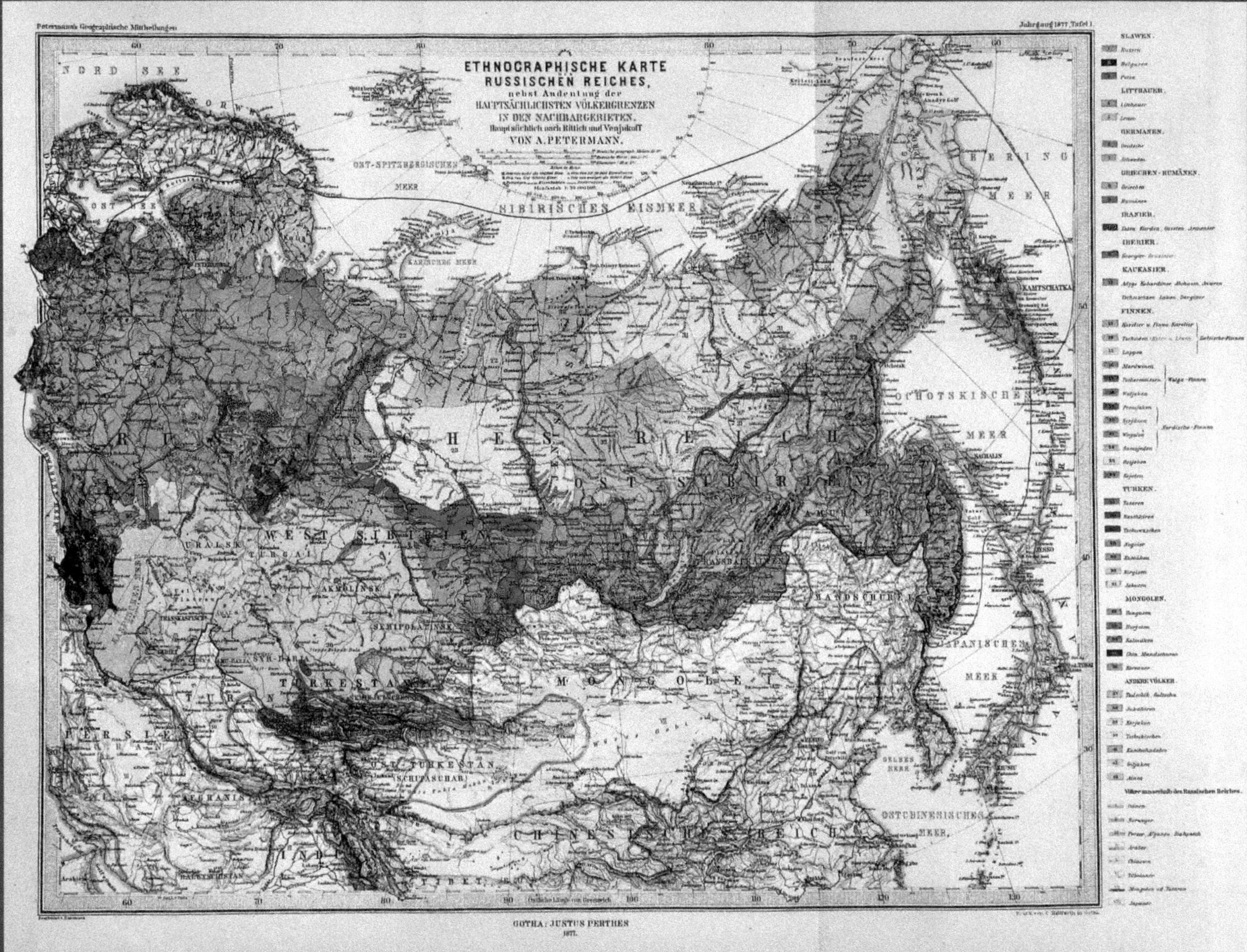
Petermann's Geographische Mittheilungen
Jahrgang 1877, Tafel 1.
ETHNOGRAPHISCHE KARTE
DES
RUSSISCHEN REICHES,
nebst Andeutung der
HAUPTSÄCHLICHSTEN VÖLKERGRENZEN
IN DEN NACHBARGEBIETEN.
Hauptsächlich nach Rittich und Venjukoff
VON A. PETERMANN.
NORD SEE
OST-SPITZBERGISCHES MEER
SIBIRISCHES EISMEER
BERING MEER
KAMTSCHATKA
OCHOTSKISCHES MEER
SACHALIN
RUSSISCHES REICH
OST SIBIRIEN
WEST SIBIRIEN
URALSK
TURGAI
AKMOLINSK
SEMIPOLATINSK
SYR-DARJA
TURKESTAN
MANDSCHUREI
JAPANISCHES MEER
MONGOLEI
PERSIEN
OST TURKESTAN
(SCHITASCHAR)
AFGHANISTAN
CHINESISCHES REICH
GELBES MEER
OSTCHINESISCHES MEER
INDIEN
TIBET
BELUDSCHISTAN
Östliche Länge von Greenwich
SLAWEN.
LITTHAUER.
GERMANEN.
GRIECHEN-RUMÄNEN.
IRANIER.
IBERIER.
KAUKASIER.
FINNEN.
TURKEN.
MONGOLEN.
ANDERE VÖLKER.
GOTHA: JUSTUS PERTHES
1877.

STEP 8

Nationality, Race, Ethnicity, Culture, and Ancestry

Some Words Are Not Interchangeable

Nationality. Race. Ethnicity. Culture. Ancestry. These five little words cause all manner of confusion when it comes to discussing different groups of people in America. They also present a conundrum to genealogy and family history enthusiasts who seek answers to three fundamental questions:

1. Who am I?
2. Who were my people?
3. To what community or communities did my ancestors belong?

From the beginning, America has been a melting pot of people from around the globe. During colonial times, groups of people came to this country and formed complex, multilayered communities. These communities have become more complex over time as more people from different backgrounds continue to immigrate to America.

In this step, we will explore how our ancestors may have identified themselves in terms of community, society, race, ethnicity, and culture. Having this information can be the difference between locating or failing to locate our ancestors in the records.

We will examine the concepts of nationality, race, ethnicity, and ancestry through a genealogical lens. Understanding these terms will give us valuable insights into how our ancestors may have self-identified as well as how others could have perceived their race.

Some of these ideas—notably, race and ethnicity—remain ever-evolving concepts. You will understand why these five terms are not interchangeable or synonymous by the end of this step.

What Is Nationality?

Nationality is a legal status that defines an individual as being part of a nation due to birth or by naturalization. It is as simple as that.

But it's not always so simple to determine the nationality of our ancestors. That's because countries change over time. Some, like Belarus, didn't exist as a nation until the twentieth century. Other Eastern European countries, like Lithuania and Poland, changed dramatically over the centuries, existing as independent nations at some points in history and as a part of Russia or other surrounding countries at others.

Understanding changing political boundaries and how the world existed in the time of a specific ancestor can affect how successfully we can find information about that person.

Now it is time to explore the concepts of race, ethnicity, culture, and ancestry. These complex concepts are often confused, conflated, swapped, or thought to mean the same thing. They are not the same, nor are they interchangeable.

What Is Race?

Race is a subjective concept and not easy to define. I especially like the definition provided by the Australian government in its *Culture, Race, and Ethnicity* lesson plan:

- Race is a term applied to people purely because of the way they look;
- It is considered by many to be predominantly a social construct;
- It is difficult to say a person belongs to a specific race because there are so many variations, such as skin color; and
- All human groups belong to the same species (*Homo sapiens*).

This subjectivity presents some core issues for genealogical researchers. For instance, early census takers working on the U.S. federal census went door-to-door and made assumptions about the race of the individuals in the households they were surveying.

> *In the colonial and early Republic periods of America's history, if you weren't perceived to be white, you were deemed to be black. It didn't matter if you were actually Native American, Asian, Middle Eastern, African, Hispanic, or of mixed ethnicity. If someone*

> *assumed that you weren't solely or primarily of European descent, you were deemed to be black. This practice presents challenges to budding genealogists. Your ancestor may have racially self-identified in one way, while a census taker could have applied a different racial category to them solely based on their appearance.*

Racial designations also changed over time as people from different backgrounds had children together. It is not uncommon to discover family lines where ancestors had changed their racial designations, going from:

- White to Native American.
- White to mulatto.
- White to mulatto to black.
- White to Native American to black to mulatto.
- Native American to black and/or mulatto.
- Black to mulatto to Native American to white.
- Black to mulatto to white.

This is something you need to consider in your research, especially if you have deep colonial American roots.

Never make assumptions about the racial classification of the person you are documenting. Follow the records wherever they lead. Make an effort to ensure that you have the correct document for the right person, and note in your research log any changing racial designation for an ancestor if it changes along the way.

What Is Ethnicity?

The Australian government's *Culture, Race, and Ethnicity* lesson plan has a concise definition of ethnicity:

- Physical characteristics, such as skin color or bloodline.
- Linguistic characteristics, such as language or dialect.
- Behavioral or cultural characteristics, such as religion or customs.
- Environmental characteristics, such as living in the same area or sharing the same place of origin.

Ethnicity refers to the shared social, cultural, and historical experiences, stemming from a common national or regional background, which make subgroups of a population different from one another. Similarly, an ethnic group is a subgroup of a community with a set of shared social, cultural, and historical experiences and with relatively distinctive beliefs, values, and behaviors.

Ethnicity is, in many ways, a *social construct*—that is, an idea that has been created and accepted by the people in a society. Ethnic membership has significant consequences for how people are perceived and treated. This is especially true for geographical communities in which people of different ethnicities have lived, worked, and married one another.

What Is Culture?

The Australian government's *Culture, Race, and Ethnicity* lesson plan has a concise definition of culture:

- It is diverse, dynamic, and ever-changing.
- It is the shared system of learned and shared values, beliefs, and rules of conduct that make people behave in a certain way.
- It is the standard for perceiving, believing, evaluating, and acting.
- Not everyone knows everything about their own culture.

Culture, it would seem, is not a fixed thing. One can move within a culture's various subcultures. That is one of the reasons why no culture can be viewed, thought about, or spoken of in absolute terms. To do so wouldn't reflect the world in which we live.

What Is Ancestry?

Ancestry is the study of a family's line of descent. Everyone has two types of descent to research, study, and document: lineal descent and collateral descent.

LINEAL DESCENT is your direct ancestral line of descent (e.g., father—son—granddaughter—great-grandson, etc.).

COLLATERAL DESCENT refers to the relationship between people who descend from the same ancestor but are related through relatives such as an aunt, uncle, cousin, or nephew.

Activity

This activity will further develop your understanding of the concepts we have explored in this step. You'll need a notebook or some loose sheets of paper.

1. On a sheet of paper, write down the culture and subcultures you belong to.
2. On a separate sheet of paper, write down the culture and subcultures your parents belong to. Jot down the different documents a genealogist could use to document their lives based on this culture and the various subcultures as well as the different places these documents can be found.
3. On another sheet of paper, write down the culture and subcultures your grandparents belong to. Jot down the different documents a genealogist could use to document their lives based on this culture and the various subcultures as well as the different places these documents can be found.

This activity will prepare you for thinking about the earlier generations of your family, the cultures and subcultures they were members of, and the kinds of documents you can access to document their lives.

Additional reading on the subject of race, culture, and ethnicity has been provided in the Resources section (page 171) to further your understanding on these topics. Spend some time thinking about these concepts. You will be applying what you learned here in Step 9 as you explore the concept of genetic inheritance.

The information you gather about an ancestor's nationality, race, ethnicity, and culture answers the *What* of the 5 Ws you must explore as part of your research. The answer to this W focuses your research by identifying the community of people your ancestor identified with and lived among.

STEP 9

Genetic and Ancestral Research: There's a Big Difference

In recent years, more and more people have been getting their DNA tested and examining their genetic genealogy. You may have done so yourself. But there are huge differences between genetic genealogy and ancestral research, and these differences will influence the type of research you want—or need—to do. This step explores these differences, concentrating on genetic genealogy versus family trees.

What Is Ancestral Line Research?

Ancestral line research is the study of a family's line of descent. It includes *lineal descent* (people who are in direct line to an ancestor, such as a child, grandchild, or great-grandchild) and *collateral descent* (people who descend from the same ancestor but are related through relatives, such as an aunt, cousin, or nephew).

Your genealogical pedigree, often depicted in a family tree, contains both your lineal and collateral family lines. In other words, your family tree includes all your biological ancestors and their siblings, aunts, uncles, and cousins.

The chart on the next page shows the number of great-grandparents we all have across the generations. Notice that we all have 1,048,576 18th great-grandparents in our direct ancestry—and that number doesn't include the siblings, aunts, or uncles of these great-grandparents!

Parents	2
Grandparents	4
Great-Grandparents	8
2nd Great-Grandparents	16
3rd Great-Grandparents	32
4th Great-Grandparents	64
5th Great-Grandparents	128
6th Great-Grandparents	256
7th Great-Grandparents	512
8th Great-Grandparents	1,024
9th Great-Grandparents	2,048
10th Great-Grandparents	4,096
11th Great-Grandparents	8,192
12th Great-Grandparents	16,384
13th Great-Grandparents	32,768
14th Great-Grandparents	65,536
15th Great-Grandparents	131,072
16th Great-Grandparents	262,144
17th Great-Grandparents	524,288
18th Great-Grandparents	1,048,576
Etc.	

As you can imagine, keeping track of so many generations can get overwhelming. That's why many researchers use a fan chart, like the one shown on page 34, to depict their ancestral family tree.

What Is Genetic Genealogy?

Your genetic genealogy is limited to the ancestors whose DNA has been passed down to you. It is crucial to understand that you do not inherit DNA from all your ancestors. The further back in time we go, the less likely we are to have inherited DNA. DNA inheritance is also random.

There are three types of DNA to consider: Y-chromosome (Y-DNA), mitochondrial DNA (mtDNA), and autosomal DNA (atDNA).

Y-DNA

Y-DNA is passed down the generations from fathers to sons. Daughters do not inherit Y-DNA. This kind of DNA is vital to confirm patrilineal descent, or descent between generations of fathers and sons in the same family line. This eliminates all the ancestors from a man's maternal side of his family.

Mitochondrial (mtDNA)

mtDNA is DNA that has been transmitted down from mothers to daughters in a matrilineal line. Mothers also pass this DNA on to their sons. Sons, however, do not pass mtDNA on to their children. In other words, mtDNA is only continuously passed down the female-to-female matrilineal line within a family.

mtDNA is not inherited from all of a woman's female ancestors. It is only passed down from mothers to daughters. This eliminates all the ancestors from a woman's paternal side of the family.

Autosomal DNA (atDNA)

atDNA is passed down randomly from generation to generation. A child does not inherit his or her parents' entire genetic makeup. Every generation loses bits and pieces of its DNA, as even siblings do not inherit the same amount of atDNA from their parents.

When it comes to cousins, the atDNA they share decreases with each passing generation that separates them. As the distance in time from a shared common ancestor increases, the likelihood of sharing atDNA decreases.

The following genetic genealogy fan chart illustrates the atDNA inheritance "lottery." The fields filled in with orange represent ancestors

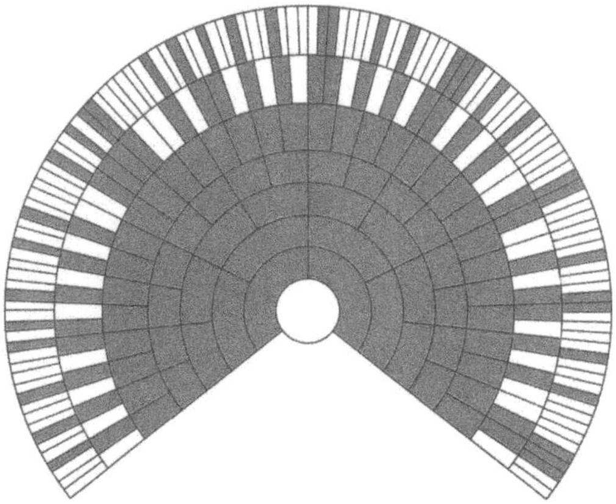

from whom a person inherited atDNA. The blank fields represent ancestors from whom a person did not inherit atDNA.

DNA and Ethnicity

DNA testing has become a popular way to discover more about our global ancestry. When you spit in a tube or swab your cheek to submit your sample, a DNA testing company will compare your DNA with DNA samples collected from populations from around the globe.

The ethnicity percentages you receive from a testing company represent the percentage of people who have a similar DNA makeup to yours. For instance, if Company A tells you that your DNA is 35 percent Greek, this means that you match 35 percent of people within Company A's database who have self-reported a Greek ancestry within the past five to seven generations.

It's important to remember that ethnicity results are not set in stone. As DNA testing companies increase their global databases of DNA, customers will see their ethnic percentages change.

While the percentages any DNA testing company provides aren't strictly accurate, they are useful. They can give you straightforward information; for example, a 70 percent Irish DNA result would not surprise anyone with known Irish ancestry stretching back many generations.

But a DNA percentage can also tell you how recently an ethnicity—especially an unexpected ethnicity—became a part of your DNA. For example, let's say the majority of your known ancestry over the past hundred years is Scottish, Irish, and Welsh. Yet your DNA test results show 30 percent Italian. That Italian DNA marker was introduced into your genetic makeup within the last few generations of your family.

Here are some other important things to keep in mind about DNA testing:

- Your DNA can tell you what countries or global regions your ancestors lived in more than 500 years ago.
- Depending on which commercial DNA company you use, you can discover when different ethnicities entered into your DNA.
- Based on the amount of DNA that you share with various peoples from around the globe, you can gain insights into how many generations ago you had an ancestor who was descended from a single population or ethnicity.
- Commercial atDNA testing companies analyze only a fraction of your atDNA. On average, commercial DNA testing companies measure only six to eight generations' worth of your DNA. In other words, you are seeing a relatively recent snapshot of your ethnic composition.
- The lower the reported ethnicity is in your DNA test report, the further back in time the ancestor who carried that ethnicity marker lived. An example would be seeing a 5 percent or less Native American ethnicity result. In this instance, the ancestor who carried a Native American DNA marker could be as far removed as a 10th, 11th, or 12th grandparent.

DNA tests can be a valuable part of your arsenal when it comes to breaking down brick walls and roadblocks in your research. We will be exploring other ways to tackle brick walls in Step 23: The Most Common Brick Walls in Research (page 73).

For a deeper understanding of DNA and how to utilize it in your research, see the material listed in the Resources section (page 171).

Search for "How to Use DNA Testing for Genealogy Research" for more assistance.

Armed with the new discoveries you've made from your ancestral line research, you will want to preserve your findings so you can share them with family members and pass your discoveries down to future generations of your family. Preserving ancestral stories is the subject we will be focusing on in Step 10.

STEP 10

Preserve and Share Your Family's Story

Every family has at least one member with a compelling a story. In the course of researching your ancestors, you've undoubtedly discovered one or more of these in your own family tree. Family history can include documents, photos, oral history, and family heirlooms. If they were lost or forgotten once, you don't want that to happen again. The following list provides some tips on how to preserve and share aspects of your family's history.

1 Create a blog and write about your family members and ancestors.

2 Record a video. Interview family members about the key events or stories in their lives.

3 Create a digital scrapbook to preserve and share memories online.

4 Convert family photos, home movies, certificates, wedding albums, CDs, etc., into a digital form that can be easily preserved and passed down.

5 Write a family history book for your family, your town, or your county.

6 Contribute your family's stories to StoryCorps, an American nonprofit oral history project, by downloading the StoryCorps app.

7 Create a Pinterest board or post your content on Instagram.

STEP 11

Access Public Information

Accessing public information is a core part of genealogical research. This may seem intimidating if it is new to you, but don't worry. This step is all about giving you the confidence to search for the records you need—and setting you up for success!

What Is a Public Record?

A public record is any document that is made or filed in the course of public business. Birth certificates, marriage deeds and licenses, death certificates, mortality schedules, court cases, land deeds, and baptism and christening records are just a few examples. Many government agencies have digitized these records and have made them available online.

Critical Thinking Will Get You Far

The first step in finding free public information is determining what kind of document you need. Understanding the 5 Ws should help you figure this out.

The 5 Ws will also help you determine the best places to search for the information you require. For instance, when researching Quaker ancestors in Pennsylvania, it wouldn't make sense to look for them in Baptist or Methodist records.

Likewise, if you are searching for information about an enslaved African American ancestor, it won't help to look in pre-1870 U.S. federal census records because these records only included people who were not enslaved. Instead, you will have to research your ancestor's last enslaver.

Are you trying to confirm a date and place of birth? Are you seeking proof of where an ancestor died? Knowing what kind of record you need and understanding why you are searching for a specific record will give you an idea of where you need to search. How you search for a record online is equally important.

Optimize Your Online Search

If you type in the search phrase "John Tyler" into Internet search engines like Google or Bing, you will face a staggering list of suggestions to view. However, if you type in a search string such as "John Tyler, Virginia, 1816 Westmoreland County will and estate inventory," you will produce a more focused list.

There is an Internet search methodology that produces even more focused search engine results: Boolean search strings.

Boolean Search Strings

A Boolean search is a way to search the Internet or databases by using keywords along with modifiers such as "AND," "OR," and "NOT." Think of this as fine-tuning or refining online searches to achieve more accurate and relevant search results.

"Yeldell" AND "Edgefield" -"John Yeldell"

The preceding example illustrates a simple Boolean search done by a researcher looking for information about some of the Yeldell family lines in Edgefield County, South Carolina. In this instance, this researcher did not want Google to return any information on John Yeldell, a famous Yeldell from Edgefield County. The researcher knew there would be hundreds of links for John, which would not be helpful. Hence the -*"John Yeldell"* in this search string. This bit of code ("-") eliminated any results that included John, which resulted in a targeted list of material and resources to view. Having this shorter list of possible information sources to sort through will save valuable research time.

For more information about how to use Boolean strings with some real-world examples, visit https://genealogyadventures.net/Boolean.

Make sure you have a firm grasp of how to access public information online, including how to use Boolean strings, before proceeding to the next subject in this step. The following five resources can familiarize you with some popular genealogical research resources where using Boolean strings will yield better search results.

Five Free Online Resources

There is a vast array of online resources for conducting genealogical research. The following list is just a sampling.

1 FamilySearch.org: This site hosts free vital records (birth, death, and marriage), U.S. federal and state census records, lineage books, family history books, religious records, probate records, African American records, and Native American records as well as parish, county, and state records and histories. http://www.familysearch.org.

2 Google Books: Google Books is an excellent resource for parish, county, and state historical and family history books, including free downloadable lineage books. https://books.google.com.

3 Internet Archive: A superb resource for free books that cover ancestry, lineage, and family history as well as local and state history books. https://archive.org.

4 JSTOR: While some of its content is pay-to-access, this online service also has millions of ancestry, family history, and lineage books you can read or download for free. If you are not affiliated with a university or are unable to access the site from a library or a Church of Jesus Christ of Latter-Day Saints genealogical center, you can sign up for free with a Gmail account. https://www.jstor.org.

5 U.S. National Archives: https://www.archives.gov.

Every state has an online historical archives website—some even have more than one. Many counties also have a historical archive, including parish records. Local, regional, and state historical societies may also have online archives. Online family associations may also have their own archives. Chances are you will have to search numerous archives to find the document(s) you are seeking.

Once you begin to collect documents, images, and other material, you'll need to think about how to store them and keep them safe. In Step 12, we'll walk through some of the ways to save photographs and digitized images so that what you have found can be shared with future generations of your family.

Т. Головинскъ

STEP 12

Save Your Photos

The story of you began long before you were born. Sharing your old family photos allows you to celebrate the power of the memories and histories that went into making you and preserve your family's legacy for generations to come.

The following list tells you how to preserve this legacy in four simple steps.

As always, you should update your research log with notes and references about the images you have found, digitized, and saved, including where they can be found within your collection of family-related materials.

1 Ask your family members

Always credit the person who gave you the photograph if you share it online.

2 Make a digital copy

Smartphone | Tablet | Digital camera | Scanner

No matter what device you use to make a digital copy, make sure that your capture quality is set to a high resolution (at least 350 dpi). Refer to your device manual for instructions on changing the resolution.

3 Name your new digital file

Include the name of the ancestor, the location, the year the image was taken, and the source in the file name. For example:
JASheffey-1872-Wytheville-JoeBloggs.jpg.

If more than one person is in the photo, use a left-to-right method to list first initials and surnames, starting with "LtR" as the first three characters of the filename. For example:
LtR-JASheffey-MASMalley-LSpiller-1891-Varina-JaneDoe.jpg.

Keep your file-naming structure consistent.

4 Save your new digital file

Flash drive | External hard drive | Laptop or desktop | Cloud storage (e.g., Dropbox) | Online family tree website | Memory card

As always, you should update your research log with notes and references about the images you have found, digitized, and saved, including where they can be found within your collection of family-related materials.

STEP 13

Create a Genealogy Timeline

A genealogy timeline is a visual way of showing the critical points in your ancestor's life, such as his or her birth and death and the birth of his or her children.

Benefits

One significant benefit of an ancestral timeline is that it may help you identify opportunities for further research. Gaps in knowledge or records will reveal themselves as you plot the key moments in an ancestor's life. Remember to add your timeline to your research log.

What to Include

A birth date and a place of birth are the obvious place to begin an ancestor's timeline, and the date and place of death will dictate the timeline's end. You can add anything you know about an ancestor's personal life for the years in between their birth and death, including:

- Date and place of baptism
- Dates and places of education
- Employment or business details
- Property purchases
- Community service
- Military service
- Marriage
- Movement between towns or emigration
- Births of any children

Once you have included an ancestor's life details, you can add local, national, and world events for more context about their life. Doing so may help you to uncover links between these events and personal experiences in an ancestor's life. For instance, you may notice that your African American ancestor left Georgia for Philadelphia in the 1920s, 1930s, or 1940s. Finding out that the Great Migration occurred throughout the American South during those decades might explain the reason for that move.

For Example

Daniel Sheffey, Sr. Timeline

BORN: CAROLINE COUNTY, VIRGINIA

AROUND 1820

What enslaver's will or deed will explain how he went from Caroline County to Wythe County in Virginia?

SLAVE MARRIAGE

1840

Relationship with Margaret Clark begins in Wythe County, Virginia (*Register of Colored Persons Cohabitating Together as Husband and Wife on 27 February 1866*).

MILITARY SERVICE: CIVIL WAR

1863

Saves the Kincannon Hotel on Main Street and the Morrison House (where he and his family were enslaved) from burning to the ground during the Union Army's raid on Wytheville in Wythe County, Virginia.

EDUCATION: HAMPTON UNIVERSITY
(formerly Hampton Normal and Agricultural Institute)

1868

Daniel and Margaret's son, Jefferson Crockett Sheffey, a former Union Army Calvary veteran, begins teaching at Hampton Normal and Agricultural Institute.

DEATH: WYTHEVILLE, WYTHE COUNTY, VIRGINIA

BETWEEN 1870 AND 1880

Daniel was alive on 12 July 1870, when he appears in the 1870 U.S. federal census. He is dead by 1 June 1880 when his wife, Margaret Clark Sheffey, states that she is a widow on the 1880 federal census.

The timeline for Daniel Sheffey, Sr. immediately reveals two areas for further research. The first is the place of his birth. His parents and siblings were all born in Wythe County, Virginia. Yet, in the *1866 Cohabitation Register for Wythe County,* he stated that he was born in Caroline County, Virginia. He may have made a mistake. If he was correct, there is a missing piece of his family's history to research further. How did he come to be born in Caroline County? Who was the enslaver of his parents who brought them to

Caroline County? How and when were they returned to Wythe County before the outbreak of the Civil War? What enslaver returned the family to Wythe County? If Caroline County was given in error, how did that happen?

The second area in need of further research is Daniel's death. There is no death record for him. An extensive search of Virginia Mortality Schedules, which predate state-mandated death certificates, has yet to uncover an entry for Daniel. All that is known at this point is that he died at some point between 1870, when he was listed with his family in the census, and 1880, when his wife, Margaret, reported that she was a widow.

Creating Your Timeline

> *The rules for creating a timeline are not set in stone. You can be as creative as you want or keep things simple and minimal. The only rule that should be followed is that a timeline should be presented in chronological order. Your timeline will no doubt change many times as your research about an ancestor deepens.*

My advice is to start by using presentation software—such as PowerPoint, Google Slides, Zoho, or LibreOffice Impress—that is easy to amend as you discover new information. Alternatively, you can begin by sketching out a timeline on paper.

Online services like Ancestry and FamilySearch automatically create timelines as you add records and information to an ancestor's page within your online family tree. You may also wish to include a timeline as part of an ancestor's research log.

Creating a timeline is a great way to visualize the key points in time during an ancestor's life. Plotting what you know and have confirmed will enable you to identify information that still needs confirmation (e.g., date of death) or information that remains to be discovered. There is information from one data source that you will want to include on your timeline: where your ancestors were living when they were listed in the U.S. federal census. We will explore the rich seam of information census records can provide in Step 14.

STEP 14

What Can Census Records Do for You?

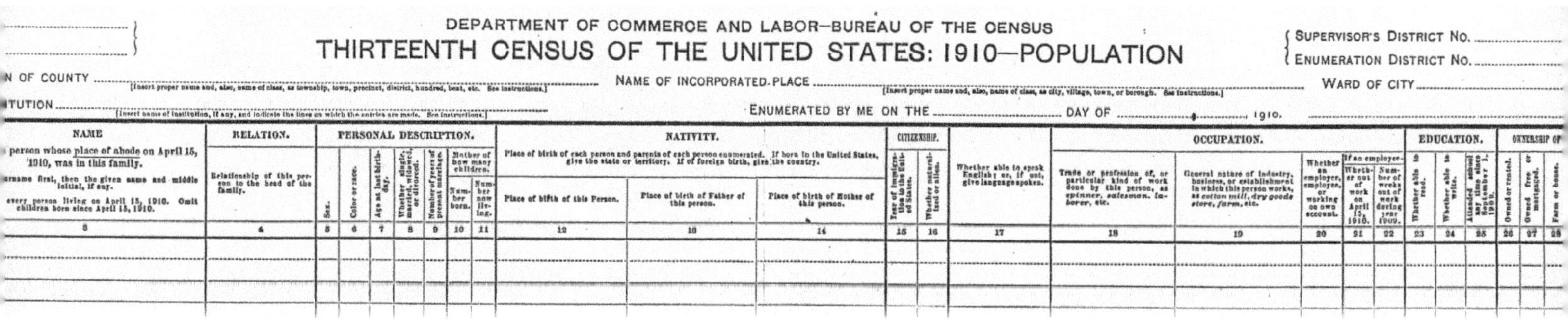

DEPARTMENT OF COMMERCE AND LABOR—BUREAU OF THE CENSUS

THIRTEENTH CENSUS OF THE UNITED STATES: 1910—POPULATION

SUPERVISOR'S DISTRICT NO.

ENUMERATION DISTRICT NO.

N OF COUNTY [Insert proper name and, also, name of class, as township, town, precinct, district, hundred, beat, etc. See instructions.]

NAME OF INCORPORATED PLACE [Insert proper name and, also, name of class, as city, village, town, or borough. See instructions.]

WARD OF CITY

TUTION [Insert name of institution, if any, and indicate the lines on which the entries are made. See instructions.]

ENUMERATED BY ME ON THE ... DAY OF ..., 1910.

NAME	RELATION.	PERSONAL DESCRIPTION.							NATIVITY.			CITIZENSHIP.			OCCUPATION.					EDUCATION.			OWNERSHIP OF		
person whose place of abode on April 15, 1910, was in this family. Surname first, then the given name and middle initial, if any. every person living on April 15, 1910. Omit children born since April 15, 1910.	Relationship of this person to the head of the family.	Sex.	Color or race.	Age at last birthday.	Whether single, married, widowed, or divorced.	Number of years of present marriage.	Mother of how many children. Number born.	Number now living.	Place of birth of each person and parents of each person enumerated. If born in the United States, give the state or territory. If of foreign birth, give the country. Place of birth of this Person.	Place of birth of Father of this person.	Place of birth of Mother of this person.	Year of immigration to the United States.	Whether naturalized or alien.	Whether able to speak English; or, if not, give language spoken.	Trade or profession of, or particular kind of work done by this person, as spinner, salesman, laborer, etc.	General nature of industry, business, or establishment in which this person works, as cotton mill, dry goods store, farm, etc.	Whether an employer, employee, or working on own account.	If an employee— Whether out of work on April 15, 1910.	Number of weeks out of work during year 1909.	Whether able to read.	Whether able to write.	Attended school any time since September 1, 1909.	Owned or rented.	Owned free or mortgaged.	Farm or house.
3	4	5	6	7	8	9	10	11	12	13	14	15	16	17	18	19	20	21	22	23	24	25	26	27	28

What did great-grandpa Joe do for a living? Where was he living in 1880? Was he an only child? U.S. federal and state census records and colonial tax lists can answer these questions—and more! Think of census records as snapshots of time. These bland-looking forms can pack quite a punch when it comes to providing superb background information about people and the communities in which they lived.

Colonial-Era County Tax Lists

Before the first federal census in 1790, American colonies had tax lists. In colonial Virginia, these were referred to as "tithable lists." These early colonial records are invaluable to genealogists. They name the head of household, along with the number of household members who were taxable, as well as taxable possessions owned by that person.

There are three crucial points to remember about tax lists:

- Only the head of the household was named, and this person was typically male.
- Each colony handled tax collection information differently.
- Census enumerators did not visit homes to collect information. Instead, heads of households submitted the information about whom and what was taxable.

Points to consider:

- Colonial tax lists only listed each person responsible for paying the tax, along with the number of "heads" for whom they were the responsible taxpayer.
- When there are multiple names listed, the first name is that of the "master or mistress of a family" (the person responsible for the tax), followed by the names or number of the taxable persons for whom that person would pay the tax. In the eighteenth century, this was males over 16 (children, overseers, apprentices, servants, and slaves) and non-white, enslaved, or indentured women over 16.
- In the case of males between the ages of 16 and 21, their parents, guardians, or masters (in the case of apprentices or servants) were responsible for the tax.
- The age of persons on the list was calculated as of June 9 of the same year. This information can be a valuable genealogical clue since the first appearance of an individual as a tithable implies the last date on which the person could have turned 16.
- Heads of households paid taxes on their indentured servants.
- Although free white women were not taxable themselves, a widow or spinster can appear on a tithable list if she was responsible for taxes on male children, servants, or slaves. Like male heads of households, she had to pay taxes for family members and non-family members of her household.
- The sequence in which names appeared within a household was usually immediate family members first and then other freemen, followed by servants or apprentices. Slaves, who were classified as taxable property, were listed last.

The U.S. Federal Census Over Time

The first federal census took place in 1790. The information requested in subsequent censuses has changed radically over the centuries. Note that language used in this timeline, such as "colored" and "idiot," comes directly from the census forms. In working with records, you must familiarize yourself with the language of the day.

- Between 1790 and 1840, census forms only noted the name of the head of household. No other family members were named. Instead, other household members were grouped according to gender and age and whether they were free white people, free people of color, or enslaved.
- In the 1820 census, free black people and enslaved people are grouped by gender and age ranges for the first time.
- In the 1830 census, heads of household were asked for the first time to provide information about the number of white persons and "slaves or colored persons" who were blind as well as the number of white persons who were non-naturalized foreigners. This census also asked for the number of people in the household who were 100 and older for the first time.
- Questions that appeared for the first time in the 1840 census include:
  - The number of persons in each family employed in specific industries, like mining, agriculture, manufacturing, and engineering.
  - Name and age of persons receiving pensions for Revolutionary or military service.
  - Number of white and colored persons who were "deaf and dumb."
  - Number of white and colored persons who were blind.
  - Number of white and colored persons who were "insane and idiots."
  - Number of white persons 20 years and older who could not read and write.
- The 1850 census was the first to list everyone in the household individually. The relationship of each individual to the head of household was not requested. The following information was also gathered in the 1850 census:
  - Color: This column was left blank if the person was white, marked "B" if a person was black, and marked "M" if a person was mulatto.
  - The profession, occupation, or trade of each person over 15. (This information is vital for genealogical research.)
  - Value of real estate and other property, place of birth, student status, literacy, and physical ability questions.
  - A Slave Schedule. (Note that Slave Schedules rarely contain names of the enslaved, listing them only by gender and age.)
- The 1860 census captured the same information as the 1850 census.
- The 1870 census is similar to those of 1850 and 1860. One difference is the inclusion of the race identifier "C" for Chinese (a category that included all East Asians) and "I" for American Indian. Again, the relationship of each individual to the head of household is

not requested. This is the first federal census where newly freed enslaved people and their families are listed individually within their respective homes.

- The 1880 census introduced several new information requests, which are important for genealogists to consider:
  - The relationship of each individual to the head of the household.
  - Each person's marital status.
  - The place of birth for each person and the place where their parents were born.
- The 1890 census returns were largely destroyed by a fire. Fragments of the census population schedules exist for Alabama, District of Columbia, Georgia, Illinois, Minnesota, New Jersey, New York, North Carolina, Ohio, South Dakota, and Texas.
- The 1900 census introduced the racial designation "Jp" for Japanese people and added the following information requests, which are all important for genealogists:
  - The number of years a couple was married.
  - For mothers, how many children she had given birth to and how many were living.
  - For immigrants, the year they immigrated to the United States, the number of years they had lived in the United States, and their naturalization status.
  - Whether a person owned their property or rented.
  - Farmers were required to provide additional information.
- The 1910 census asked further questions about a person's profession and employment status. It also asked whether the head of household was a survivor of the Union or Confederate Army or Navy. An Indian Population Schedule was also introduced in 1910.
- The 1920, 1930, and 1940 censuses don't differ too much from the 1910 Census. The questions about the number of children a woman had and how many were still living were omitted.

More information about the U.S. federal census, including blank forms for each year and a full list of the questions that were asked on each census form, can be found on the U.S. Census Bureau website: https://www.census.gov/history/www/through_the_decades.

State Censuses

State censuses were taken in the years between the federal censuses. State census records may be found in a variety of locations, including state archives, state historical societies, state libraries, the Church of Jesus Christ of Latter-Day Saints' Family History Library, or on the Internet. While they do not capture the depth of information provided on the federal census, state census returns are also an invaluable source of information.

For African Americans researching their formerly enslaved ancestors, state censuses taken between 1866 and 1869 are a gold mine of information. They mark the first time newly freed enslaved people were listed within their respective households.

Cohabitation Lists for Formerly Enslaved People

Starting in 1865, the Bureau of Refugees, Freedmen, and Abandoned Lands (the Freedmen's Bureau) created lists of newly freed enslaved people who were living as man and wife, along with their children. These lists vary from county to county and from state to state. Some include the names of a person's last enslaver, which is invaluable information. Some also include the ages of everyone in the household, from which you can work out their year of birth. The information may also include the places where the head of household and his or her spouse were born as well as the approximate number of years they had cohabitated. These records may be found in local courthouses, state archives, and libraries.

You can access these records and discover more about the information they contain by visiting the FamilySearch.org website.

Federal and state census records, and Cohabitation Lists offer you a window into your ancestors' stories, as well as clues about new family members to add to your family tree.

STEP 15

Explore Marriage Records

Ready to dive into your ancestors' relationships? Marriage records offer a treasure trove of information to help you answer many of the 5 Ws.

Local laws usually required that marriages be recorded in civil records, regardless of whether a civil or church authority performed the ceremony.

Typically, the clerk of the town or county where the bride resided stored the marriage record. However, marriage records—particularly early ones—can also be housed in state archives. You can find more recent marriage documents in a state's Vital Records Division.

A word about marriage indexes: These are transcriptions of the original document. Indexes will only contain the bare minimum of information. When possible, it is always best to locate and review the original marriage document.

The example at the right highlights the differences between a marriage index and a marriage record.

Here is the information contained in the text index file for Daniel Sheffey's marriage certificate:

NAME	Daniel Sheffey
GENDER	Male
MARRIAGE PLACE	Franklin, Virginia, USA
SPOUSE	Emma Turnbull

Here is the original marriage certificate:

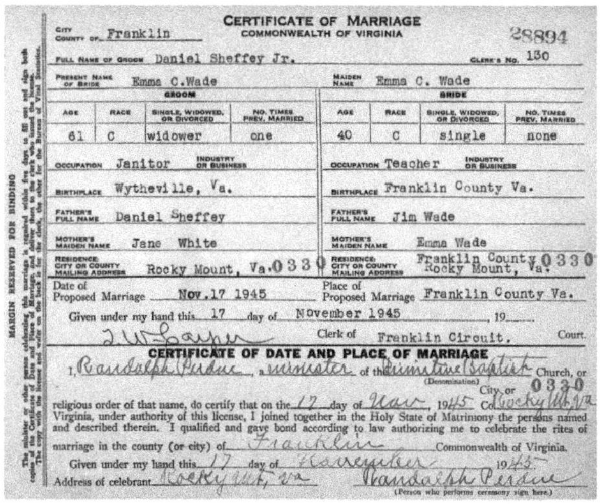

CERTIFICATE OF MARRIAGE
COMMONWEALTH OF VIRGINIA

City / County of Franklin — 28894

Full Name of Groom Daniel Sheffey Jr. — Clerk's No. 130

Present Name of Bride Emma C.Wade — Maiden Name Emma C. Wade

GROOM				BRIDE			
Age	Race	Single, Widowed, or Divorced	No. Times Prev. Married	Age	Race	Single, Widowed, or Divorced	No. Times Prev. Married
61	C	widower	one	40	C	single	none
Occupation	Janitor	Industry or Business		Occupation	Teacher	Industry or Business	
Birthplace	Wytheville, Va.			Birthplace	Franklin County Va.		
Father's Full Name	Daniel Sheffey			Father's Full Name	Jim Wade		
Mother's Maiden Name	Jane White			Mother's Maiden Name	Emma Wade		
Residence: City or County, Mailing Address	Rocky Mount, Va. 0330			Residence: City or County, Mailing Address	Franklin County, Rocky Mount, Va. 0330		

Date of Proposed Marriage Nov.17 1945 — Place of Proposed Marriage Franklin County Va.

Given under my hand this 17 day of November 1945, 19__

Clerk of Franklin Circuit. Court.

CERTIFICATE OF DATE AND PLACE OF MARRIAGE

I, Randolph Perdue, a minister of the Primitive Baptist Church, or (Denomination) 0330 religious order of that name, do certify that on the 17 day of Nov, 1945 City or Co. Rocky Mt, Va Virginia, under authority of this license, I joined together in the Holy State of Matrimony the persons named and described therein. I qualified and gave bond according to law authorizing me to celebrate the rites of marriage in the county (or city) of Franklin Commonwealth of Virginia.

Given under my hand this 17 day of November 1945.

Address of celebrant Rocky Mt, Va — Randolph Perdue (Person who performs ceremony sign here.)

MARGIN RESERVED FOR BINDING

The minister or other person celebrating this marriage is required within five days to fill out and sign both copies of the Certificate of Date and Place of Marriage, and deliver them to the clerk who issued the license. The copy with the license and wafer on the back is for the clerk, the other for the Bureau of Vital Statistics.

Note how much more information can be gleaned from the original document compared to the index file for the same record.

> *You can request a copy of a marriage certificate by contacting the Vital Records office in the state where the marriage occurred. A state's Vital Records office website will have instructions on how to request a copy as well as information on any applicable fees. You may be required to submit information about yourself and why you are requesting the document.*

Records of an Intention to Marry

Beginning in the 1600s, parishes and counties created various records to show a couple's intention to marry.

Marriage Banns

Marriage banns were a public announcement of a couple's intention to marry. This practice was common in the Southern and New England colonies and states from the 1600s through the mid-1800s. Traditionally, the announcement of an impending marriage was read out in a place of worship in the three-week period before the wedding ceremony. Marriage banns gave the community where the couple lived an opportunity to raise any objections to the marriage.

Banns were then presented to the local civil authority and posted in a public place.

These announcements were recorded in a register by the minister or town clerk and can sometimes be found today with other town or church records.

Marriage Bonds

Marriage bonds were written guarantees or promises of payment and were presented to the minister or official who would perform the ceremony.

The groom was responsible for arranging the bond. Sometimes a bond was made by someone other than the groom, like a relative of the bride. The person who posted the bond was referred to as the surety or bondsman.

These records were frequently used in the Southern and mid-Atlantic states through the mid-1800s.

Consent Papers

If the bride or groom was underage, the consent of a parent or a legal guardian was required. Parental or guardian consent may have been given in written or verbal form for the license or bond. These legal documents can also be found in the town or county clerk records.

Marriage Contracts or Settlements

Contracts or marriage settlements were documents created for the protection of legal rights and property for the bride, groom, or both. These legal documents were occasionally a part of a marriage application, especially in American regions that were colonized by France or Spain. Marriage contracts were also used by wealthy colonists and can sometimes be found in state archives and repositories.

Applications and Licenses

Applications and licenses are the most modern types of records showing an intention to marry, as they have come to replace old forms of marriage records, such as banns and bonds. A license is obtained by making an application to the proper civil authority, like a parish, town, or county clerk. The information that is provided—such as the couple's names, ages, and places of residence—holds crucial genealogical information. More modern twentieth-century marriage records also provide details about race, birth dates, and occupations and usually include the names of the bride and groom's parents.

Items You May Discover in a Marriage Record

- Church of marriage ceremony
- County where the marriage took place and the residence of the bride and groom
- Dates and/or locations of births as well as ages for bride and groom
- Marriage date
- Full names of bride and groom
- Bride's maiden name
- Names and birthplaces of the bride and groom's parents
- Names of the bondsman or witnesses to the marriage, who were often relatives
- Occupation of the groom
- Marital status of the bride and groom (single, widowed, or divorced)

Where to Look for Marriage Records

- Church records
- Parish, county, and state archives
- Local and state historical societies
- City and county civil registries
- Family Bibles and personal histories
- Google and other Internet search engines
- Google Books
- Newspapers
- Online records sites, such as Ancestry, FamilySearch, HeritageQuest, and MyHeritage.
- Genealogies posted online at:
  - Genealogy.com
  - GenealogyLinks.net
  - MyTrees.com
  - Rootsweb.com
  - WikiTree.com

Of particular note for those whose ancestors may have been enslaved people newly freed during or after the Civil War in the United States is the Freedmen's Bureau Marriages (1861–1872) collection on FamilySearch.org. These records consist of unbound marriage certificates, marriage licenses, monthly reports of marriages, and other proof of marriages, mostly for newly freed enslaved people.

As you've probably gathered, marriage records can provide quite a backstory. Take your time as you read through your ancestors' marriage records. A thorough reading will answer some of your 5 Ws and reveal something of the world in which your ancestor lived. You may want to preserve the backstory a marriage record reveals by ordering a copy of the original document to add to your research log or files. We will be exploring how to order copies of original records next in Step 16.

DO NOT WRITE ON THIS SIDE

ALL BLANKS BELOW ARE FOR USE OF COUNTY RECORDER

PLACE OF MARRIAGE — County of Los Angeles

California State Board of Health

State Index No.

BUREAU OF VITAL STATISTICS

STANDARD CERTIFICATE OF MARRIAGE

Local Registered No. 19993

PERSONAL AND STATISTICAL PARTICULARS

GROOM		BRIDE	
FULL NAME	John Harrison Huddleston	FULL NAME	Jo Elizabeth Stafford
RESIDENCE	1717 No. Bronson, LA	RESIDENCE	5269 DeLongpre, LA
COLOR OR RACE	white	COLOR OR RACE	white
AGE AT LAST BIRTHDAY (Years)	25	AGE AT LAST BIRTHDAY (Years)	19
SINGLE WIDOWED OR DIVORCED	single	SINGLE WIDOWED OR DIVORCED	single
NUMBER OF MARRIAGE	1st	NUMBER OF MARRIAGE	1st
BIRTHPLACE (State or country)	Farmer City, Illinois	BIRTHPLACE (State or country)	Coalinga, Calif.
OCCUPATION (a) Trade, profession, or particular kind of work	Singer	OCCUPATION (a) Trade, profession, or particular kind of work	Singer
(b) General nature of industry, business, or establishment in which employed (or employer)	Radio	(b) General nature of industry, business, or establishment in which employed (or employer)	Radio
NAME OF FATHER	Clyde E. Huddleston	NAME OF FATHER	Grover C. Stafford
BIRTHPLACE OF FATHER (State or country)	Farmer City, Illinois	BIRTHPLACE OF FATHER (State or country)	Gainsboro, Tenn.
MAIDEN NAME OF MOTHER	Ollie McDonald	MAIDEN NAME OF MOTHER	Anna J. York
BIRTHPLACE OF MOTHER (State or country)	Farmer City, Illinois	BIRTHPLACE OF MOTHER (State or country)	Gainsboro, Tenn.

MAIDEN NAME OF BRIDE, IF SHE WAS PREVIOUSLY MARRIED

We, the groom and bride in this Certificate, hereby certify that the information given therein is correct to the best of our knowledge and belief.

John H. Huddleston, Groom — Jo E. Stafford, Bride

CERTIFICATE OF PERSON PERFORMING THE MARRIAGE

I Hereby Certify that John Harrison Huddleston and Jo Elizabeth Stafford were joined in marriage by me in accordance with the laws of the State of California, at Hollywood this 15 day of October 1937

Signature of Witness to the Marriage: Charles Mason

Residence: Hollywood

Signature of Person Performing the Ceremony: Scott Anderson

Official position: Minister

Residence: Hollywood, Calif.

FILED Oct 21 1937 C. L. LOGAN, Recorder, Registrar (County Recorder) By B Moran, Dep

A full, true and correct copy of the original recorded this 21st day of Oct 1937 at 9 A.M.

C. L. LOGAN, Recorder,

By Jane O'Leary, Deputy

M Scharf, Deputy County Clerk

If filled out in the presence of

DO NOT WRITE ON THIS PAGE

ALL BLANKS ABOVE ARE FOR USE OF RECORDER

STEP 16

Examine Vital Records

Vital records help you meet the Genealogical Proof Standard by providing key pieces of genealogical-related information. These records of a person's life events are filed and maintained under local and state governmental authority. Vital records include:

- Birth certificates
- Marriage licenses (or marriage certificates). In some places, marriage-related records may also include records of civil unions or domestic partnerships.
- Probate records
- Mortality schedules, which were a part of federal censuses from 1850 to 1880, counted the individuals who had died in the previous year.
- Death certificates

In general, vital records weren't kept in the United States until the early 1900s. At a minimum, they usually contain the full name of the individual involved in the event as well as the date and location where the event took place.

Many vital records contain much more information. For example, birth records usually list the full names of the baby and the parents as well as the date and location of the birth. Marriage records often include the names and birthplaces of each individual's parents, and divorce records usually list the names of the couple's children. Death certificates often mention where the individual will be buried and also give the name of the individual who reported the death.

Requesting a Copy of a Vital Record

You can request a copy of a vital record by contacting the Vital Records office in the state where the document is filed.

Look for detailed, state-by-state information about how to access and obtain vital records on the VitalRec website at http://vitalrec.com.

Vital records are crucial to answering the 5 Ws of your research while meeting the Genealogical Proof Standard that you learned about in Step 5: Document Your Research (page 17). Don't forget to include the information you learn from these documents in your timelines as well as in your research log.

Records like the ones you have explored in this step may also provide a glimpse into your family's broader heritage. Vital records generated by Quaker communities, for instance, paint a vivid cultural picture of their religious community. Bear in mind the link between vital records and heritage as we explore the world of heritage in Step 17.

STEP 17

Explore Your Heritage

Genealogical research provides a foundation for exploring your heritage. Hopefully, your genealogical research will uncover information about the countries from which your immigrant ancestors and enslaved African ancestors originated. Once this is known, you should be able to find cultural, historical, pictorial, and travel books that cover the cultures and ethnicities that are a part of your family's history.

8 Ways to Explore Your Heritage

1 Take a DNA test to discover your various ethnicities.

2 Read about the history of your different ethnicities.

3 Cook a meal in celebration of your ethnic cultures.

4 Learn to speak your family's native language.

5 Attend cultural and ethnic events.

6 Host a foreign exchange student or an international student.

7 Create a music playlist with music from your family's country or culture of origin.

8 Visit your family's country of origin.

Which one of these explorations can you undertake now? Don't forget to add the information and discoveries you find to your research log.

Part of your family's heritage may include its relationship to the land and land ownership. Perhaps owning a small farm was an age-old dream back in the Old Country? If land was a factor in your family's decision to move to the United States, you may find the next step particularly helpful, as we walk through how to access land records.

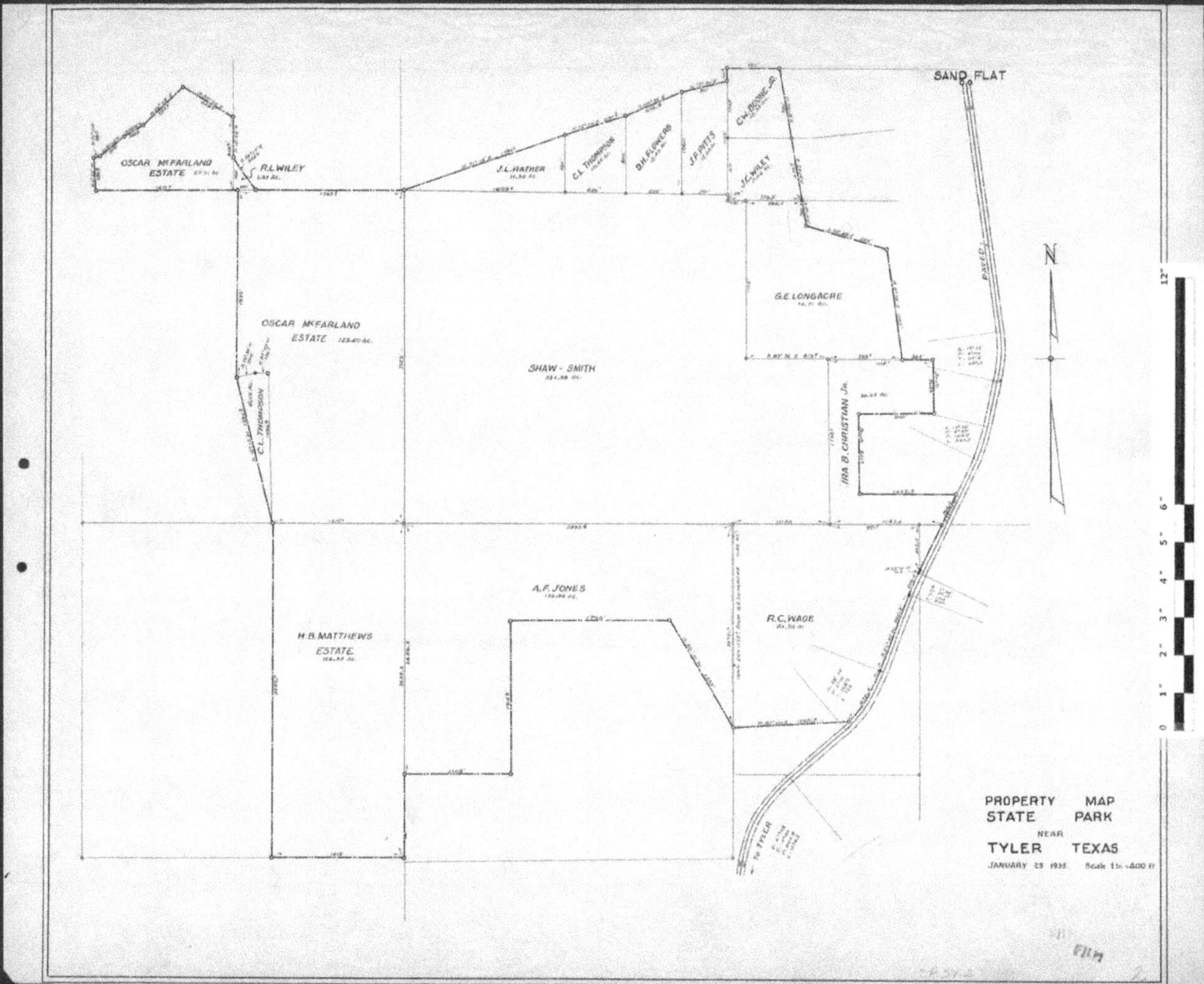
SAND FLAT
OSCAR McFARLAND ESTATE
R.L. WILEY
J.L. RATHER
C.L. THOMPSON
D.H. FLOWERS
J.P. PITTS
C.W. BOONE JR.
J.C. WILEY
G.E. LONGACRE
OSCAR McFARLAND ESTATE
SHAW - SMITH
IRA B. CHRISTIAN Jr.
C.L. THOMPSON
PAVED
N
A.F. JONES
R.C. WADE
H.B. MATTHEWS ESTATE
To TYLER
PROPERTY MAP
STATE PARK
NEAR
TYLER TEXAS
JANUARY 29 1935 Scale 1 in = 400 ft
FILM

STEP 18

Access Land Records

How much land did your ancestor own? Who were his or her neighbors? The answers can probably be found in land records.

Broadly speaking, there are two types of land classification: State Land States and Public Land States. Each class provides useful genealogical information, but the information differs. You will need to access them differently, too.

State Land States versus Public Land States

State Land States

State Land States (SLSs) are defined as the 20 colonies and states that did not relinquish the unclaimed land held within their borders to the federal government when they became part of the United States. SLSs include the original 13 colonies plus Kentucky, Maine, Tennessee, Texas, Vermont, West Virginia, and Hawaii.

You will need the name of the person who purchased the land, the patentee (the person with the legal right to sell the land), the county where the land was owned, and the approximate transaction date. One clue that you are looking at an SLS land transaction is the way in which boundaries are described. For instance, you might see a boundary drawn with squiggly lines running from an old oak tree past Jacobson's Swamp and over to Pope's Creek. In other words, you will see references to natural landmarks describing a non-rectangular or non-square tract of land.

You can find State Land States land grants in state archives. You may also find these records in local and state historical and genealogy societies.

The Five Basic SLS Property Transfer Documents

1 The application: A request for a warrant to have a survey made, usually a slip of paper.

2 The warrant: A certificate authorizing a survey of a tract of land. A warrant initiated the title of the property.

3 The survey: A hand-drawn sketch of boundaries for a tract of land with the exact total acreage listed.

4 The return: An internal, administrative property description document that was sent from the Surveyor General to the Secretary of the Land Office.

5 The patent: The final, official deed from the colony, commonwealth, or state, which conveyed a cleared title and legal rights to the private owner.

SLS land records generally will not provide extensive genealogical information about a land purchaser. For example, you are not going to find personal data such as the person's place of birth, age, marital status, or occupation. However, SLSs can be used to document the presence of an ancestor in a specific place at a given time.

Tracking Down Public Land Records

Public land records are not held in a single repository or location. There are two main locations that house these records:

Western States

Tract books are located in the National Archives Building in Washington, DC. This includes the following states: Alaska, Arizona, California, Colorado, Idaho, Kansas, Montana, Nebraska, Nevada, New Mexico, North Dakota, Oklahoma, Oregon, South Dakota, Utah, Washington, and Wyoming.

Eastern States

The Bureau of Land Management (BLM) holds the tract books and patents. This includes the following states: Alabama, Arkansas, Florida, Illinois, Indiana, Iowa, Louisiana, Michigan, Minnesota, Mississippi, Missouri, Ohio, and Wisconsin.

Public Land States

There are 30 Public Land States formed from the public domain. These states are Alabama, Alaska, Arizona, Arkansas, California, Colorado, Florida, Idaho, Illinois, Indiana, Iowa, Kansas, Louisiana, Michigan, Minnesota, Mississippi, Missouri, Montana, Nebraska, Nevada, New Mexico, North Dakota, Ohio, Oklahoma, Oregon, South Dakota, Utah, Washington, Wisconsin, and Wyoming. There are over 10 million individual Public Land State (PLS) land transactions held by the National Archives.

Unlike SLSs, PLS records contain information with a specific interest to genealogists. PLS records document the transfer of public land from the federal government to private ownership. The genealogical value of these records is based on the range of information they provide, such as the land buyer's age, place of birth, military service, citizenship, literacy, and land use, and they may also include information about family members.

The depiction of a consistent, orderly, rectangular survey system based on ranges and townships is one clue that you are looking at a PLS land transaction.

Related Land Records

It may take a substantial amount of research and digging into land records to find the land your ancestor once owned. However, the effort involved in locating an ancestor's land records is worth it. You may find a treasure trove of information about your family that you will never forget. As always, don't forget to log your discoveries!

Survey Notes and Field Plats

Survey notes and field plats can be found in local, state, and university archives and local and state libraries as well as in historical and genealogical society collections.

Survey plats are drawings of boundaries prepared by draftsmen based on data from land survey sketches and field notes.

U.S. Military Bounty-Land Warrants

The U.S. federal government provided bounty land for those who served in various wars between 1775 and 1855, including:

- The Revolutionary War.
- The War of 1812.
- The Mexican-American War (1846–1848).
- Wars with Native American nations.

Donation Lands

To attract settlers to the remote territories of Florida, New Mexico, Oregon, and Washington, the federal government offered donation land grants to individuals who would agree to settle there and meet a residency requirement. Donation lands were a precursor to homesteading.

Homesteads

Under the Homestead Act of 1862, settlers were given 160 acres of land in the public domain if they built a home on the land, resided there for five years, and cultivated the land. This land did not cost anything per acre, but the settler did pay a filing fee.

Your ancestors may have received land as a reward for military service. For instance, fighting in the American Revolution was one way many colonial men became landowners. We will be exploring other discoveries you can make from military records in Step 19.

STEP 19

Retrieve Military Records

An ancestor's military service is often a source of family pride. Feats of derring-do, bravery, sacrifice, and heroism are great stories fit to get passed down through generations. These stories also have the added benefit of getting your family members interested in the research you are doing!

Military personnel records are primarily administrative and can contain the following information:

- Muster, enlistment, and appointment dates
- Military rank and date of rank attainment
- Duty stations and service assignments
- Training, qualifications, and performance
- Awards and medals
- Disciplinary actions
- Officer and administrative remarks
- Separation, discharge, or retirement causes and dates

To locate a military service record, you must provide basic information including the veteran's complete name as used in service, their service number, Social Security number (if applicable), the branch of service in which they enlisted, dates of service, and date and place of birth. Records are available for service personnel who separated from the military more than 62 years ago.

Obtain military records through the National Personnel Records Center (NPRC) or by visiting the U.S. National Archives website. Records held by the NPRC or the National Archives will be subject to a copying fee.

> *Records of individuals who left military service less than 62 years ago are subject to access restrictions, as the current legal provisions limit the amount of information that can be released about a veteran to the general public. These limitations may also affect the amount of information that can be disclosed in copies of military records for veterans who left military service more than 62 years ago.*

Older service records may also be obtained through the online commercial company Fold3, which covers individuals who served in the following conflicts:

- American Revolution
- War of 1812
- Mexican-American and Early Indian Wars
- Civil War
- Spanish-American War
- World War I
- World War II
- Korean War
- Vietnam War

Retrieving military records is a straightforward process, and the information you gather will fill in some of the gaps you uncovered with your notes on the 5 Ws. These records can also really bring your ancestor's life story home in a gripping and exciting way.

Most of the time, you will be able to find the military records you need online. However, you may be missing an opportunity by not visiting a brick-and-mortar location like an archive to expand your search for military records. In Step 20, we'll weigh the benefits of online research versus on-site research.

COMPREHEND

STEP 20

Genealogy Research: In Person versus Online

The availability of billions of digitized records from around the world has revolutionized genealogy. However, billions more have not been digitized. At some point, you will have to visit a brick-and-mortar building that houses genealogical records to further your research.

While you can accomplish much via the online route, always keep in the back of your mind that at some point you will need to visit a repository, library, courthouse, etc., to access original documents to learn more about an ancestor's life.

In-person visits are great for another reason, too. Chances are the original records are kept in a place where your ancestor and his or her family lived. Combine your research time with some sightseeing so you can see the community they were a part of. You can walk in your ancestors' footsteps. You never know, the old family house may still be standing!

Exploring the locale your family comes from makes for some memorable moments. We will take a peek at some of the other ways you can explore your local history in Step 21.

Key Differences between Online and In-Person Research

	Online Searches	In-Person Searches
Number of documents	➤ Billions of genealogical documents are available. ➤ Documents are downloadable and easy to attach to individuals in a family tree.	➤ Billions of genealogical records have not been digitized. They can only be accessed by visiting in person or by requesting staff to digitize and send you specific documents (which often requires a fee). ➤ Access to non-digitized records requires visiting the place where they are stored, digitizing them (with permission!), and archiving them.
How complete is the information?	➤ Some digitized records only provide a fraction of the information from the original document (e.g., index files).	➤ Original on-site records contain all the original information, including handwritten notes that can lend important context.
Information errors	➤ Transcriptions of original records may contain omissions, typos, and misspelled names that compromise the value of the information that has been published.	➤ Apart from name spelling variations or errors provided by firsthand informants, original documents are the most accurate source of information.

	Online Searches	In-Person Searches
Access to professional support	• Commercial genealogy websites often have limited free professional support. • You may have to do a separate online search for professionals or specialists who can assist you, and they often charge a fee.	• In-house state archival and research staff can assist you for free. • In-house local historical society or genealogical staff can assist either for free, for a small fee, or for the cost of a membership.
Access to subject experts	• Access to individuals with subject expertise is limited. • In most cases, you will need to do your own online search for a local, regional, or state expert.	• In-house subject experts are available to assist you with your research. • In-house staff can point you to local, regional, or state experts who can provide additional resources or research materials.
Ability to provide contextual or historical information	• Access to contextual information is very limited. • In most cases, you will need to do your own online search for a local, regional, or state expert who can offer historical context.	• In-house subject experts can assist you by adding context to a document or a historical event. • In-house staff can point you to local, regional, or state experts who can provide the additional historical context that you require. • In-house staff are more likely to suggest additional avenues, information sources, or approaches for your research.

STEP 21

Explore Local History

Researching the local history of the town or city where your ancestors lived is a great way to understand the people, places, and events that impacted the course of their lives. Following are some suggestions for exploring local history to add context to your ancestors' lives.

READ PUBLISHED LOCAL HISTORIES

- You can find town and county histories in your local library, historical society, or genealogy society or online.

FIND LOCAL MAPS

- Old maps of a city or town often include details such as residents' names and property locations. You may discover who your ancestors' neighbors were! Look for city and county atlases, survey maps, and plat maps, which are available online or in various archives.

EXPLORE LOCAL, STATE, AND UNIVERSITY LIBRARIES

- These libraries often house information not available elsewhere. Your local library may hold local published histories, directories, and collections of local records. Ask the research librarian about the genealogy reference section. State and university libraries may store historical manuscripts and newspaper collections.

ACCESS COURT RECORDS

- Property disputes, proposed road layouts, probate records, civil complaints, and estate inventories are all rich sources of information about a family and the community in which they lived.

CHECK OUT HISTORICAL LOCAL NEWSPAPERS

- Business notices, arrests, local politics, obituaries, death notices, court cases, marriage announcements, town events, school activities, and society columns offer a glimpse into the daily lives of local residents. A newspaper's public announcements and advertisements tell us about important activities and social customs of residents' lives at the time.

REACH OUT TO LOCAL GENEALOGICAL AND HISTORICAL SOCIETIES

- Genealogical and historical societies will also contain local history books, records, and family genealogies not found in other places. Staff are local history and genealogy enthusiasts and professionals, offering a depth of information that will be useful in learning about the community in which your ancestors and their families lived. Learning about the places where your ancestors lived will help you understand their lives more deeply. Without this information, you will have an incomplete picture of their lives.

One way of bringing local history home is through maps, which we'll explore in Step 22.

PARADE GROUND
E. 17TH ST.
E. 18TH ST.
E. 19TH ST.
WAVERLY AVE
OCEAN AVE.
CHURCH LANE
CATON
CROOKE
IRVING PLACE
CLARKSON AVE
FRANKLIN AVE.
BROOKLYN & FLATBUSH ROAD
UNION PL.
LOCUST ST
UNION ST
VERNON AVE
LOTT ST.
JOHNSON ST.
EAST BROADWAY
MARTENSE AVE
LINDEN BOULEVARD
RIDGEWOOD AVE
DIAMOND ST.
PROSPECT ST
SHERMAN ST.
BUTLER ST.
GRANT ST.
ERASMUS ST.
LLOYD ST.
LAWRENCE ST.
Judge John A. Lott
John C. Bergen
Heirs of David E. Clarkson
Hrs. of D. E. C.
Gen. Philip S. Crooke Res.
U. A. Murdock S. B. Chittenden & Wm. H. Taylor
Henry Johnson Est.
Mary Wall
Wm. Matthews
ST. PAULS EPIS. CH.
Ref. Dutch Ch.
REF. DUTCH CH. CEMETERY
WILLINK HOUSE
Brooklyn City R.R. Co.
Phebe Duryea
Jane Duryea
Anna Duryea
Gertrude Jewitt
ERASMUS HALL ACADEMY
SCHOOL NO. 1
M.E. CHURCH
Theodore A. Lott
Henry Lyles Jr.
J. V. Schoonmaker Res.
Adrian Vandeveer Res.
J. A. Vandeveer
Miss Mary Vandeveer & Others
Napoleon Kulvirk
Ref. Dutch Ch.
O. G. Walbridge
Louis P. Griffith
T. Flood Est.

STEP 22

Make Use of Maps

Maps aren't an obvious genealogical research tool, but they can be very helpful in locating:

- The town or area where your ancestor lived.
- Where families who shared the same surname and lived in the same town were living in relation to one another.
- Ancestral migration patterns.
- Towns, cities, and counties that no longer exist.
- Changes in colonial territorial boundaries to understand where your ancestors lived in specific time periods.
- Changes in parish, county, and state boundaries to know where your ancestors lived in a particular time period.
- Land your ancestors owned.

The Best Maps for Genealogical Research

The FamilySearch Wiki page suggests the following maps for genealogical research:

- Atlases
- Census maps
- Chamber of Commerce maps
- City and town maps
- County, parish, territorial, or state maps
- Fire insurance maps
- Land ownership maps
- Military maps
- Railroad maps
- Maps in old newspapers
- Topographic maps

Look for "Map Genealogy" on the FamilySearch website for more information on using maps in your research.

Useful Map Resources

Historical maps can be found online as well as in brick-and-mortar repositories like libraries. Following are some online collections with which you should familiarize yourself. All are easy to find via Internet search engines.

- American Memory Map Collections, from the Library of Congress
- Atlas of Historical County Boundaries Project
- Perry-Castañeda Library Map Collection, at the University of Texas at Austin
- David Rumsey Historical Map Collection, which contains 79,000 historic maps
- Historic Map Works
- Library of Congress Maps, grouped by place, collection, subject/topic, date and more
- Old Maps Online

Maps can provide some answers to the 5 Ws of research. You may want to keep a reduced-size copy of your maps in your research log.

Maps may also do something else. They might just help you break through a stubborn brick wall, a topic we'll be exploring in Step 23.

COMPREHEND

STEP 23

The Most Common Brick Walls in Research

As you make progress in your family-history research, you are likely to encounter a few setbacks. Some may feel more like brick walls. These are frustrating and disheartening, I know. I've run into them myself—often. In fact, brick walls are par for the course in genealogy. Take comfort in knowing that your frustrations are shared by others, and never fear because this step offers some handy workarounds for tackling those pesky brick walls.

First, understand that a genealogical brick wall is often composed of two things:

- An End of Line (EoL) ancestor
- A lack of information about that EoL ancestor

An EoL ancestor is an ancestor for whom we cannot identify or verify parents. When there are no records to prove an ancestors' parents or siblings, location of birth, etc., you've hit a brick wall.

11 Common Reasons for Brick Walls

1 **Record loss by fire** Courthouses and other local or state government administrative buildings catch fire and burn down, destroying all or most of the documents they housed.

2 Burnt counties Counties experiencing multiple conflicts over time can result in the burning of buildings that housed local or state records.

3 Changing surnames You may find that some of the families you are researching changed their surnames. Searching for a family with the same first names and similar birth years is one way to crack this kind of brick wall. You may also find the new name your ancestor used by seeing if they were still living near the same families in concurrent census returns.

An additional marriage for a female ancestor may be a reason why you cannot find her after a certain date. You may be looking for her under one married name when she in fact died with a new surname from a later marriage.

4 Name spelling variations
On the road to becoming the surname you recognize today, your surname may have undergone one or more iterations. People who were the first in their family to read and write often spelled their names phonetically. A surname like Roane could become Rone, Rhone, or Rowan. Regional accents also influenced the phonetic spelling of a last name. It is also worth remembering that standardized name spellings weren't commonplace until after the early nineteenth century.

Family feuds could also lead to surname spelling variations—for example, with one brother spelling his surname "Reid," another spelling it "Reed," and a third brother choosing "Redd."

5 Relocation Sometimes an ancestor and their family seems to have disappeared from the face of the earth, when in fact, they just relocated. One way to break through this kind of brick wall is to search for another family in a different location that has the same names and birth years as your research subjects. Additional research will help you determine whether the two families are indeed the same people or not.

Another consideration is whether your ancestor died in prison or in a state mental health facility. Prison and state hospital records are also important sources of genealogical information.

6 Use of first and middle names
Your ancestor may sometimes have used their first name and sometimes their middle name, depending on the document, so you may need to search under both.

7 Nicknames Some ancestors went by nicknames—for example, Polly for Mary, Patsy for Martha, Bob for Robert, and Will, Willie, or Wiley, for William. You will need to familiarize yourself with the most common nicknames used when your ancestor was alive.

8 War Battles and conflicts are one of the most overlooked reasons why an ancestor or their family seemingly disappeared. Were they killed or captured? Were they removed to another place? Removal is a crucial factor for conflicts involving Native American and frontier ancestors. Research the local history for battle dates in the places where your ancestors lived to answer this question.

***9* Slavery** Enslaved African-descended Americans rarely produced firsthand information for documents and records. Secondhand accounts and information provided by third parties about enslaved people form the documented evidence for the lives of the enslaved. In essence, every enslaved ancestor is an EoL ancestor who requires deep research in order to break the brick wall they represent. This is not the same for European indentured servants, who were listed by name on indenture contracts and ship manifests.

***10* Changing racial designation** Multiracial colonial families created a multilayered tapestry of descendants. Descendants who were fair-complexioned enough to assume a white identity might have altered the family surname to break ties with their black and mulatto cousins while still desiring to acknowledge something about their origins. This is how the tri-racial Virginia and North Carolina Cumbo family produced white Cumbee and Cumbie descendant lines in the Southern states.

***11* Changing ethnic identity** Your ancestors may have opted to alter their surname to obscure an old ethnic identity or to adopt a new one.

Government Records and Brick Walls

Document transcription errors are common. Names can be written down incorrectly or omitted entirely. This is one reason original documents are essential.

This is a critical reason why researchers read every digitized record they find very closely. Did the transcriber include all the household members in that 1880 federal census? Did the enumerator write Frances instead of Francis or Jessie instead of Jesse for a male in the household? Did they put stepchildren down with the surname of their stepfather rather than their correct surname?

> *Information could have also been entered incorrectly on an original document. Clerks are, and were, human. For instance, a clerk could have misheard a name and spelled it incorrectly, making it difficult for you to prove that the document you're looking at is the correct one. Due diligence, more in-depth research, and critical thinking are all necessary when locating and accessing records you believe are associated with an ancestor you are researching.*

Overcoming Brick Walls

Before you can break through a brick wall, you'll need to go back over all the research you've done so far. There may be something you've overlooked or forgotten to include.

If you haven't done so already, make sure all your research has been recorded in your research log. Then:

1 Research the siblings and close cousins of your brick-wall ancestor. This may provide the missing information you need, such as the name of a parent or a mother's maiden name.

2 Organize, review, and evaluate the evidence you have collected.

3 Summarize or restate the problem you are experiencing.

4 Review all the old sources and resources you have collected for overlooked clues.

5 Separate your assumptions from what you have confirmed in the documents you have for that ancestor.

6 Use critical thinking to sort and weigh the evidence at hand and then analyze that information for relevance, the directness of the evidence, transcription errors, accuracy of data, believability of the source, the likelihood of the event, and consistency with other proven facts.

7 Update your research log to clarify your thinking.

8 Document why you searched where you did, what you found or did not find, and what that means in terms of reevaluating future research strategies for your EoL ancestor.

9 Write down what possible sources of information should be searched next, why, how long that will take, and the likelihood of success.

In the words of the television series *The X-Files,* the truth is out there. It's our job to think of all the means we have at our disposal to find that information. The nine suggested steps for overcoming brick walls are all tried and tested approaches that can lead to a breakthrough. There is one especially common brick wall genealogists often face: tackling the origin story for an immigrant ancestor. In Step 24, we'll address researching ancestors' roots in other countries.

STEP 24

Conduct International Research

Searching for your ancestors back in the Old Country can be an exciting part of genealogical research. You may gain a better sense of your origins, learn about different customs, or maybe even learn a new language. There is even a possibility you will connect with long-lost cousins who may become lifelong friends!

> *The types of international records and resources you find will vary from country to country. As with researching in the United States, you will have to familiarize yourself with the different kinds of records available for the country that your ancestors originally called home. You needn't worry about learning to be fluent in a new language. Official documents will be in a format standardized to that country. You will only need to recognize a few crucial words, such as "name," "birth," "death," "father," and "mother," to unlock the information contained in official international documents.*

Essential Items to Consider

- Begin by interviewing family members such as parents, cousins, aunts, and uncles about your family's origins. Some of the information you gather may be contradictory. That's okay. Focus on those kernels that are consistent to begin your search.

Florenz 1. 9/3. 08 – L. M. diese Karte gilt auch
für Schr. S. Ich hatte mir bereits Montag [illegible]
[illegible] als 2 letzten Tage in Venedig waren
recht kalt u. ungemütlich, so daß wir vorzogen
nicht erst auf Bologna zu bleiben u. sind
gestern Sonntag früh um 10 mit Walter's u.
Schwester Ida bis hier gefahren haben ein Coupé
[illegible] wir hatten die Fahrt nach Bologna
[illegible] viel [illegible] Kastanienhainen
und Maulbeerbäumen [illegible]
Venedig [illegible] hier hatten wir 46 Tunnel
zu durchfahren. Nach der Wasserscheide des
Adriat. u. Tyrrhenischen Meeres
wird es nach der Seite auffallend
milder u. ich glaube über [illegible]
[illegible] blühen [illegible]. Wir sind
gestern Nachmittag 5 Uhr erst in der
Stadt in einem Hotel abgestiegen
befanden uns aber [illegible] schlecht dort
u. gingen suchen nach einer bekannten
Pension. Wir haben diese nun seit heute
Montag Mittag: Pension Fioravanti
Via Solferino 5. hier bleiben wir vielleicht
7 Tage ([illegible] hier [illegible] Stadt
nicht) sind sehr gut untergebracht u. [illegible]
allerdings [illegible] Schrank [illegible]
zu Tisch meist Engländerinnen u.
Italienerinnen. Signora Fioravanti spricht
französisch auch ein wenig [illegible]
[illegible]
[illegible] Fenster [illegible]
[illegible] gegenüber ein [illegible]
Garten mit Orangenbäumen mit
reifen gelben Orangen voll besetzt [illegible]
[illegible]
zahlen [illegible] 7 Lire täglich. [illegible]
[illegible] K! [illegible] allen herzl. Grüße Nora.

- Check your ancestor's immigration records for details about their country of origin. If your immigrant ancestor arrived after 1860, check federal census returns to see what information they provided about the country they left when they arrived in the United States. Alternatively, see the country of origin their children provided about their parents in census returns for 1880, 1900, 1910, 1920, and 1930.
- Prepare yourself for seeing a different language and gauging how much of it you may need to learn.
- Always remember that the surname you are researching may have changed over time (e.g., from Scheffe and Shoeffe in Germany to Scheffy, Sheffie, and Sheffey in America).
- Understand how historical shifts in international borders will affect your research and know when these boundary changes occurred.
- Old documents mean old forms of writing. With ancient British records, for instance, you will have to grapple with a type of old cursive writing that is difficult to read as well as archaic forms of languages, such as Old English.
- Learn about all the information resources that are available in that country, such as government records, university libraries, and genealogical societies.
- The Church of Jesus Christ of Latter-Day Saints (LDS) has International Family History Centers all over the world. Locate the LDS Family History Center in the region of the country you are researching. Alternatively, you can contact the head LDS Family History Center in the country where your ancestors originated. This organization will put you in touch with local genealogists and historians who will help you with your research for a fee or for free.
- Hire a local researcher/historian.

International records can provide a rich backdrop to your family's history. Conducting international research can lead you to exploring your heritage by traveling to the cities, villages, or towns where you ancestors lived before they arrived in America.

Don't forget to update your research log with the research avenues you will need to explore as well as any discoveries you make. Make sure that you include the names of the resources you have found, the information they contain, where they were stored, and how you accessed them (e.g., a website URL or library location).

STEP 25

Cite Sources

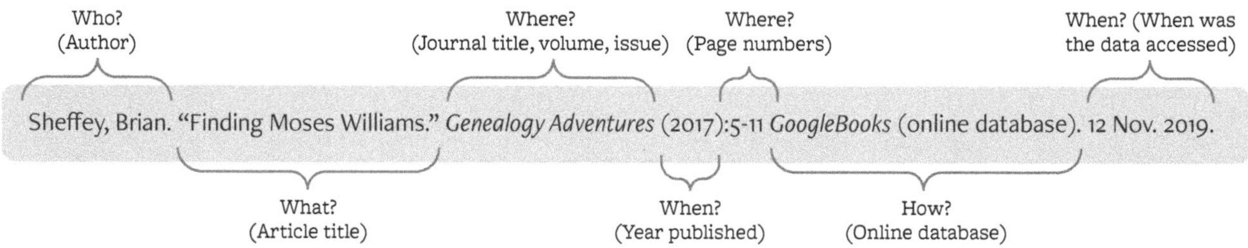

Why Cite Sources?

It is vital to maintain and keep track of every piece of information you gather when researching your family as well as every source for that information. Information sources verify the data you have found. Other researchers will use the source you have provided to review your information and to confirm that the documents you used are associated with the correct person. This is crucial when there is a conflict in informational sources.

> *Without citing sources, could you tell another researcher where you found the birth date for your third great-grandfather? Was it from his tombstone? Was it from a family Bible? Family lore? The 1880 census? A book? Or did you copy it from another family tree? If your third great-grandfather didn't provide his birth date, then who did? What was that third party's source for this information? How likely is it that they would have known his date of birth? Citing sources answers these question and many more.*

Remember: Any statement of fact, whether it is a birth date or an ancestor's surname, must carry a source that another researcher can reasonably access.

Researchers use source citations to:

ASSIST OTHERS IN VALIDATING YOUR RESEARCH. Providing citations enables others to gauge whether you understand and use the genealogical standards of good research practice.

REVISIT OLD EVIDENCE. You may discover new information that brings up additional questions, requiring you to backtrack through your original research findings. If you've cited your sources, you won't have to rely on your memory.

RECORD THE LOCATION OF EACH PIECE OF DATA. Part of genealogical best practices is specifically noting where a piece of information came from so another researcher can locate it.

CITE ANOTHER RESEARCHER'S WORK. If you relied on data supplied by a previous researcher, you must note where that previous researcher found that piece of information. What source of information did he or she use to document that piece of information? Where is that information source located?

PROVIDE CONTEXT. This allows other researchers to evaluate your data. Context also will enable you to evaluate a document itself and the information and evidence that you have gathered from it. This practice is essential for addressing any inferences or potential biases in your research.

PICK UP WHERE YOU LEFT OFF. Life has a way of taking us away from our research. Routinely citing sources saves researchers hours of trying to figure out what stage they were in before real life interrupted them.

> *Remember to note whether the source of information you have used was a primary (firsthand) source or a secondary source. Secondary, derivative sources are transcribed, abstracted, translated (from an original language), or summarized from an original. If you need to refresh your memory regarding these terms, please revisit Step 1: The 5 Fundamental Ws of Research (page 1) and Step 6: Develop a Research Outline (page 20).*

2 Rules for Great Source Citations

1 Follow the formula While there is no scientific formula for citing every type of source, a good rule of thumb is to work from general to specific:

AUTHOR. The person(s) who wrote the book, provided the interview, or wrote the letter you have used as proof for an ancestor.

TITLE. If it is an article, then the title of the article, followed by the title of the periodical;

PUBLICATION DETAILS. The place of publication, name of the publisher, and date of publication, written in parentheses (Place: Publisher, Date) as well as the following:

- Volume, issue, and page numbers for periodicals
- Series and roll or item number for microfilm
- Where you found it—repository name and location, website name and URL, cemetery name and location, etc.
- Specific details—page number, entry number and date, and date you viewed a website

2 Cite what you see Whenever you use a derivative (secondary) source instead of the original version, you must take care to cite the index, database, or book that you used and NOT the actual source from which the derivative source was created. Remember, derivative sources are several steps removed from the original, opening up the door for errors.

Even if a fellow researcher tells you that they found a certain date in a marriage record, you should cite the researcher as the source of information while noting where they claim to have found the information. You can only accurately cite the marriage record if you have viewed it for yourself.

For your assistance, a list of citation formats has been provided for you in Appendix B: Citation Formats by Information Source Type. Don't forget to add your research sources and citations to your research log!

Citations keep your research organized, and they will save you time. One type of source you will absolutely want to include in your log is newspaper articles. In Step 26, we'll explore how newspaper research can take your genealogy to the next level.

STEP 26

Use Newspapers in Genealogical Research

Newspapers can provide a gold mine of information about your ancestors. Publications from the colonial and early Republic periods can be accessed in state-level archives, historical societies, and specialist repositories. Newspapers will be either in paper format or stored on microfilm. You may also find old publications online via services like NewsBank's Readex database and the Library of Congress's Chronicling America or by using a search string like "colonial-era newspapers archive."

What are some of your ancestor's life experiences you might discover?

1 Birth notices

- Confirms birth name
- Confirms parents
- Confirms date and place of birth

2 Death notices and obituaries

- Confirms date and place of death
- Confirms immediate and extended family members and where they were living at the time the person died

Columbian Centinel.

WHOLE NO. 2,618.] BOSTON, (Mass.) SATURDAY, MAY 6, 1809. [[illegible]

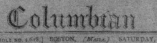

Columbian Centinel.

POLITICAL, MERCANTILE, AND MISCELLANEOUS.

PUBLISHED WEDNESDAYS AND SATURDAYS, BY BENJ. RUSSELL, DEVONSHIRE-STREET, [illegible]

New Advertisements.

Aqueduct Corporation.

[illegible]

FABER'S VIEW OF THE PROPHECIES.

[illegible]

HURD on the Prophecies.

[illegible]

The Young Dey of Algiers.

[illegible]

Pimento and Pork.

[illegible]

New Advertisements.

Nolen & Gridley,

RESPECTFULLY inform their friends and the Public, that they have opened [illegible]

Freeman & Cushing,

[illegible]

S. J. Prescott,

[illegible]

Haven, Williams & Co.

[illegible]

Trott & Blake.

[illegible]

Fresh Goods.

[illegible]

Fettyplace and Watson,

[illegible]

Hussey & Barker,

[illegible]

Adams & Wood,

[illegible]

George Pierce,

[illegible]

Israel Munson,

[illegible]

Sugar, Coffee, &c.

[illegible]

Brandy, Feathers and Flour.

[illegible]

Green Coffee.

[illegible]

New Advertisements.

NOTICE.

RICHARD EDWARDS, informs his friends and the public that he has Removed from No. [illegible], Long-Wharf, to [illegible]

Removal.

JAMES FERARI, Ladies' and Gentlemen's fashionable HAIR-CUTTER and HAIR DRESSER, [illegible]

Invoice Goods per Albatross.

[illegible]

American Manufacture.

[illegible]

Public Accommodation.

[illegible]

THE WARREN TAVERN, IN CHARLESTOWN.

[illegible]

Wharf and Stores.

[illegible]

Exchange on New-Orleans.

[illegible]

Boston:

THURSDAY, MAY 4, 1809.

[illegible] FROM ENGLAND—LATE.

The ship Mary Ford has arrived in Halifax, from Liverpool, and brought London papers to the 23d March—five days later.

The Duke of York had resigned the Command of the British Army; and the duties of Commander in Chief were to be discharged by Gen. Sir David Dundas, until an arrangement on that head could be made by Parliament.—It was expected the office in future would be exercised by Lords Commissioners, as that of Lord High Admiral now is.

The news from Spain was to the 25th February, not so late as we have received direct. The massacre and imprisonment of some Spanish officers, in an insurrection at Cadiz, was detailed, and lamented.—[We have before received accounts of this insurrection.—A people, contending, as the Spaniards are, for Freedom and Self-Government, driven almost to desperation, and fearing and feeling the insidious poison of French intrigue and influence destroying the vitals of their Revolution, may be expected at times to depart from a correct line of conduct, and to cast momentary shades on the cause of True Patriotism.] The French were detested; and the English greatly caressed by the Spaniards in Cadiz. The Globe, of the 23d March, 9 o'clock, P. M. stated, that the Telegraph had just announced, that a Courier was on the road with important despatches from Spain. [illegible]

MASSACHUSETTS AGRICULTURAL SOCIETY.

[illegible]

Massachusetts Representatives.

[illegible]

REPRESENTATIVES—CHOSEN 1809.

[illegible]

CORRESPONDENCE.

[illegible]

MORE OF ADAMS' LETTERS.

[illegible]

3 Engagement and wedding notices

- Confirms date and place where the couple lived
- Confirms the names of their family members
- Confirms date and place where the couple married

4 Military service notices

- Muster lists
- War service
- Draft board notices and lists

5 Local awards, school awards, and sports news

- A great way to add some depth and color to an ancestor's life. Were they a great student? A star athlete? Were they active in their community?

6 Community social events

- From community gatherings to notices about out-of-town family paying a visit and family reunions, social event news articles can provide nuggets of pure gold!

7 Religious community news

- From church fetes to celebrations of a religious community's founding, these articles add context about an ancestor's religious and community life.

8 Local scandals

- Not every ancestor led a quiet life. News reports covering duels, fights, feuds, affairs, riots, etc., can yield important ancestral clues.

9 Business news and local advertisements

- A great way to find out more about the family business!
- Lawsuits and government petitions
- Did Great-Grandpa Joe petition his local parish for a new road? Did siblings fall out over an inheritance? Discover the things that occupied your ancestors' lives.

10 Property transactions

- Property-related articles can confirm the date and place where your ancestor lived. You can also gain clues about when they may have left an area.

11 Local history articles

- Whether it's a family lineage article or an article about a pioneer ancestor, local history articles can provide answers for many of your genealogical questions.

While vital records and census records are essential for building the foundation of your genealogical research, don't overlook newspapers. They can hold some amazing—and sometimes quite sensational—information.

Using Boolean search strings will keep your newspaper searches more focused. Refer back to Step 11: Access Public Information (page 37) for more information about Boolean searches.

Official documents such as census records and vital records were created based on standardized forms, which included a limited number of questions. Newspaper stories are different. While journalists would have been guided by a specific topic, like announcing which men had to report to the local draft board, they were relatively free to include whatever details they felt were relevant. Some of that additional contextual information can be genealogy gold.

Learning about what was happening in the time and place an ancestor lived in will help you begin to flesh out the research you've done and create a captivating story of their life.

If you descend from a family of color, newspaper articles can provide some incredible information about your family. With that in mind, it's time for us to take an introductory look at African American genealogy research.

STEP 27

Begin African American Research

African American genealogical research presents a unique set of challenges, but as a result, it can be some of the most rewarding research to do. Stitching together a disrupted family tree can reunite long-lost branches of a family split apart by slavery, or you may discover the vibrant communities that free people of color built over generations. Whether they were enslaved or free, this step introduces you to some primary considerations you will need to think about as you begin researching your black American ancestors.

The 3 Strands of African American Research

When it comes to researching African American ancestry, there are three strands to consider: (1) the period from the 1870 federal census to the present, (2) enslaved African American ancestors, and (3) free people of color. Each strand requires you to view your ancestors through a different lens, as each lens will assist you in identifying the specific records you will need to access to uncover their stories and histories.

Let's explore each of these strands.

Strand 1: From the 1870 Census Onward

To research African American ancestors from the 1870 federal census until the present day, you simply need to follow the previous steps in this book. You will access the same types of records, such as marriage certificates, birth records, death records, military records, and newspaper articles. Be sure to include the following often-overlooked sources of black genealogical information:

- African American newspapers, which are available online via the African American Newspapers Collection, Ethnic NewsWatch, ProQuest, and Readex.
- Student records held by Historically Black Colleges and Universities (HBCUs).
- Railway service records, available via Pullman Employee Records online and the National Archives in Washington, DC. Alternatively, you can do a simple Internet search for service records held within your state archives.

Strand 2: Enslaved Ancestor Research

Researching the enslaved may be daunting, time-consuming, and intimidating for those new to this kind of research; however, it is not impossible. Critical thinking and out-of-the-box reasoning are crucial to finding the footprints that enslaved ancestors left behind.

The principle difference in researching enslaved ancestors is that the records that document their lives are secondary, not primary, sources of information. Slave records contain information *about* enslaved people and not information *from* enslaved people. You must think about:

- The kinds of records on which an enslaved ancestor's name might appear.
- Where that document would have been filed.
- Where you are most likely to find these records today, if they still exist.

How can you determine if an ancestor's family was enslaved? The 1870 census is vital. First, you must find out where your ancestor and his or her family were listed as living in the 1870 census. Were they landowners or renters/sharecroppers? If the family owned the land they resided on, try to find them in previous census years in the same town or county. If you locate the same head of the household in the 1860 census, please move on to Strand 3: Free People of Color.

If you can't find the same head of the household in the 1860 census, you will need to begin researching the family as enslaved people, which includes:

First, identify whose land they were living on if the family did not own the property in the 1870 census. The landowner may have been the family's last enslaver. In this instance, try to find a Freedmen's Labor Contract for your ancestor and the landowner. You can access these contracts, as well as bank records and cohabitation records, on the FamilySearch website. These resources provide a wealth of genealogical information about newly freed enslaved people after the end of the Civil War.

> *Look for "Freedmen's Bureau Labor Contracts, Indenture, and Apprenticeship Records, 1865–1872," "Freedmen's Bank Records, United States, Freedmen's Bureau Marriages, 1861–1872," and the "1865 and 1866 Cohabitation Records" at https://www.familysearch.org/en/.*

Secondly, identify the last enslaver of your ancestor. You may be able to identify the last enslaver by examining the numerous records in the "United States Freedmen's Bureau, Records of Freedmen, 1865–1872" section of FamilySearch. You may also find this information via a variety of resources, including:

- Historical accounts published in local history books, sometimes also available online.
- State and county archives and historical society archives.
- Specialist repositories.
- Legal suits, which can be found in state libraries or county courthouses.

Baptism, christening, and marriage records may also exist for enslaved ancestors. The availability of these kinds of records for enslaved people will depend on whether the enslaving family routinely formalized these events.

Researching a Slave-Holding Family

Once you have identified an ancestor's last enslaver, you will need to research that enslaver's family. Vital information is contained in wills, codicils, estate inventories, and estate administrative papers (collectively referred to as probate records); farm or plantation ledgers; and journals, slave insurance records, etc. These documents can help you identify the enslaver's family member and also provide clues about how enslaved family members and their descendants were treated by the enslaving family over the generations.

Strand 3: Free People of Color

Researching free people of color (FPoC) works much in the same way as researching all non-enslaved people. FPoC can be found in census records from the first census in 1790 onward. Before the 1790 federal census, FPoC are listed in county tax lists. Probate, military, marriage, and court records may also exist for ancestors who were FPoC. You may even find baptism records, too.

> **What Does Free People of Color Mean?**
>
> *FPoC was a legal designation codified in American colonial law in the 1600s. A person was legally classed as an FPoC via three*

> *routes. The first route was being born to a white, black, or mulatto mother who was legally free at the time her child was born. The legal status of the father was not a factor. Children of an enslaved father and a free mother had the legal designation of being a FPoC.*
>
> *The second route was something called manumission, the legal process by which an enslaver set their enslaved people free either while they were alive or in their will after they passed away. Surviving manumission files can be found in county courthouses or state archives.*
>
> *The third route to being designated a FPoC occurred when enslaved people contested their enslaved status through the courts in what are called manumission suits.*

There are additional FPoC-specific records you will need to access, including:

Freedom papers and certificates of freedom, which proved the free status of a person and served as a legal affidavit. These papers were filed in county courthouses. Not every colony or enslaving state mandated freedom papers. Those that did included Delaware, the District of Columbia, Maryland, and Virginia. Northern colonies that required freedom papers were New Jersey and Pennsylvania.

Manumissions and emancipations, which were official legal documents that formalized the act of setting a black person free from slavery by a living or deceased slaveholder. They are housed in state archives or local court archives.

> *Look for resources on researching FPoC on the Genealogy Adventures website at https://genealogyadventures.net/*

African American research is a vast topic. The depth of this subject is too broad to be covered in a single step of this book. Fortunately, there are trusted and well-respected online broadcasts and podcasts by some of America's top African American genealogists that cover this subject in great detail. These include the *African Roots Podcast*, BlackProGen, and Genealogy Adventures as well as many of the podcasts and shows on Blog Talk Radio.

African American genealogy presents a unique set of challenges, as you have explored in this step. However, it is far from impossible to achieve success. In this step, we've covered a variety of resources available for your African American research. In Step 28, we will talk about an additional avenue to explore: community-level organizations. These historical and genealogical societies, libraries, and specialist local repositories hold a treasure trove of information about African American families.

STEP 28

Identify Community Support

Hidden away within your local community are individuals who possess a wealth of knowledge about local families and provincial history. In this step, you will explore three of the primary sources of local community support: research librarians, local historical societies, and local genealogical societies.

Benefits of Local Research Support

Research Librarians

A research librarian is a library specialist who is employed by a college, research library, or large local library that houses in-depth information on a particular subject.

> *Most librarians are not genealogists. While they want to help you, they generally don't have the time or inclination to get involved in your research. They will show you the books or files and how to use the computer/copier/microfilm machine and perhaps recommend other research resources, but they will not do your work for you.*

The front desk at your local library will be your first point of contact. If the library has a research librarian or genealogy librarian/specialist, a staff member will refer you to that person. If not, the staff should be able to tell you which nearby libraries do. To save time, it's a good idea to phone ahead to sort this out. You can also find lists online featuring the largest or best genealogy libraries in each state and country.

Preparing for Your First Research Visit to the Library

Your first task will be to locate your nearest library and find out if there is a research librarian on staff. Many local libraries have a website, so try researching this online first. Alternatively, you can search your state library's website, which may have a list of local libraries in that state with links to their websites. You can also find information on social media, including Facebook, Twitter, Instagram, and various blogs.

If you cannot find anything online, you can call or email the library. You can usually find an address and a phone number on the county's website. Do remember that public libraries are sometimes run by volunteers, so it may be challenging to get your questions answered.

Before you visit the library, determine if:

- They have a genealogy or local history collection.
- There is anyone available to assist you with their collection.
- There are any restrictions on using the materials.
- There's a best time to visit.
- They have any special or unique items.

Once you've located a library with a research librarian, consider calling in advance to give him or her a chance to prepare for your visit.

What You Should—and Should Not—Ask on Your First Trip to the Library

One question that you should avoid asking is "I'm new to genealogy; can you help me?" Instead, take some time to form specific goals and questions ahead of time.

For instance, you may have discovered when your great-grandfather was born but not where. Your goal would be to find the location of his birth. Your question for the research librarian could be "What sources of information can you point me to that might help locate my great-grandfather's birthplace?"

Similarly, you can ask if the library has old newspapers for a specific date if you know your ancestor died on that day in that area.

If you are at the library because you know or suspect you had family in that area, it is appropriate to say you are looking for information about a specific family. You don't need to add any details. Reference librarians are trained to ask questions designed to draw out what you are seeking. Don't be offended when they ask questions about your goals or family. They are not trying to pry; they are just trying to help.

Local Genealogical and Historical Societies

Family history societies and genealogical societies are organizations that allow members to accumulate and share local knowledge. Large societies may own a library, and they may even sponsor research seminars, publish journals, or arrange international research trips. Some societies may concentrate on a specific niche, like a geographical area, ethnicity, nationality, or religion. Lineage societies limit their membership to descendants of a specific person or group of people of historical importance.

Reasons to consider joining a society include the following:

NETWORKING. Membership provides opportunities to meet and share information with people who are undertaking similar research. You might find people willing to answer questions about records or particular research problems. Some members may be available to provide research assistance, for a fee, for out-of-county and out-of-state researchers.

CONFERENCES, WORKSHOPS, MEETINGS. Societies often host conferences, genealogical research skills workshops, monthly meetings, and annual meetings. Activities vary from member presentations about their research and lectures by professional genealogists and history professors to webinars, live-stream events, and educational opportunities.

JOURNALS AND PUBLICATIONS. Many societies will have books by local or regional authors and historians plus journals and publications that are not available elsewhere.

MEMBERS-ONLY ACCESS. Many societies will have libraries and databases that are only accessible by their members. These resources will be free to members. Smaller societies may also have a library that may be available as a special collections room or collection within a public library.

Meeting up with local historians and genealogists is one of the bonuses of doing in-person research. They are natural-born storytellers. You may come away with a tale or two that will leave your family spellbound!

Remember, to better achieve your desired outcome, develop a succinct, clearly articulated information request before you meet with a reference librarian.

One final thing to consider in terms of local support: Are there local historians and authors who have blogs where they share stories or information about local history? In Step 29, you will explore how to identify blogs that are trustworthy and deserve your time and attention.

STEP 29

Identify Worthwhile Blogs

There are tens of thousands of genealogy-related blogs on the Internet. Some of them are professional, while others have been created by enthusiasts or hobbyists. So how do you know which ones to trust or spend a considerable amount of time on and which ones to avoid? In this step, we explore how to determine if the blog you've found is one you can trust.

My advice is to take a little bit of time to explore the blog or website and critique it using the guidance provided here.

Sources

Where does the blogger's information come from? Is it based on scientific research?

- Credible websites, like books and scholarly articles, should cite the source of the information presented.
- Look to see if—and how—sources are cited for key pieces of information.
- Quality of source(s): What type of source is primarily used (e.g., a respected historian or a Wikipedia article)?

Links

Are there links to and from other reliable genealogy sites?

- Type the URL into the search box on Alexa.com. Click on "Get Details." Learn about the site's traffic info, who is linking to them, and other details.

Author

Who runs or created the site? Can you trust them?

- Does the author use their name on their blog, or is it a pseudonym?
- What are their credentials?
- Does their writing show personal biases, or do they use sources and citations to support their findings?
- Can you communicate with the owner of the site?
- Check their LinkedIn profile for subject relevance and credibility.

Independent

Who runs and pays for the site?

- Is it sponsored by a large organization?
- What is the site promising or offering?
- How does the site collect and handle personal information? Is the site secure (e.g., uses https:// instead of http://)?
- Are you reading news—or advertising?

Date

When was the information presented written or reviewed? Is it up-to-date?

- Subject recency
- Is the site updated frequently?
- By including a date, a blog allows readers to make decisions about whether its information is recent enough for their purposes.

STEP 30

What's a Pioneer Certificate?

During your research, you may have discovered that you have an ancestor who was an American pioneer—one of the early settlers in the Midwest or Western territories.

Proving your connection to a pioneer can be an exciting way to honor the adventure-filled spirit of your ancestor. Pioneer Certificates are offered by several genealogical societies to the direct descendants of pioneers. Generally, these societies recognize the descendants of people who settled in a place before a specific date.

To learn if a society in your state or county issues these certificates, enter the search phrase "[State name] pioneer certificate" in your favorite search engine. If your state-related search doesn't yield any results, try searching for "[County name] pioneer certificate."

You will have to prove your connection to pioneers by using resources such as church records; birth, marriage, and death certificates; or territorial census records. You may be asked to submit a pedigree chart, and a small fee may also be charged (usually less than $15).

Pioneer certificates are an interesting feature to include in your family tree and research log and to share with your family.

STEP 31

Research Naturalization Records

With the exception of Native Americans, the United States is a country of immigrants—many of whom eventually became citizens. Unless you're researching Native American ancestors, at some point you'll need to access immigration and naturalization records. These documents will give you interesting insights into details such as whether your ancestors traveled alone or with family members and how old they were when they made the journey.

As with other records, naturalization records can also answer some of your 5 Ws.

Where Can I Find Naturalization Records?

Pre-1906 Naturalizations

Naturalization is the process by which an immigrant becomes a citizen.

Before 1906, any municipal, county, state, or federal court of record could grant United States citizenship to an immigrant. (A court of record is a trial court or appellate court in which a record of the proceedings is captured and preserved for the possibility of appeal.) A few indexes and records have been donated to the National Archives from counties, states, and

THE UNITED STATES OF AMERICA

ORIGINAL
TO BE GIVEN TO
THE PERSON NATURALIZED

No. 4746970

CERTIFICATE OF NATURALIZATION

Petition No. 137504

Personal description of holder as of date of naturalization: Age 49 years; sex Male; color White; complexion Fair; color of eyes Brown; color of hair L.Brown; height 6 feet 1 inches; weight 160 pounds; visible distinctive marks Lame right hip
Marital status Divorced; former nationality British

I certify that the description above given is true, and that the photograph affixed hereto is a likeness of me.

Sign here

Sam Dalziel Heron
(Complete and true signature of holder)

EASTERN DISTRICT OF MICHIGAN
SOUTHERN DIVISION } ss:

Be it known, that Sam Dalziel Heron
then residing at The Whittier, Burns Dr., Detroit, Mich.
having petitioned to be admitted a citizen of the United States of America, and at a term of the District Court of The United States held pursuant to law at Detroit on Sept 30 1940 19
the court having found that the petitioner intends to reside permanently in the United States, had in all respects complied with the Naturalization Laws of the United States in such case applicable, and was entitled to be so admitted, the court thereupon ordered that the petitioner be admitted as a citizen of the United States of America.

In testimony whereof the seal of the court is hereunto affixed this 30th day of Sept. in the year of our Lord nineteen hundred and forty and of our Independence the one hundred and sixty-fifth.

(T... SO AS TO COVER A PORTION OF THE LOWER EDGE OF THE PHOTOGRAPH)

Seal

GEORGE M. READ
Clerk of the U. S. District Court.
By [signature] Deputy Clerk.

DEPARTMENT OF LABOR

local courts and are available as National Archives microfilm publications. However, as a general rule, the National Archives repository and database don't have naturalization records created in state or local courts.

Contact your state archives to request a search of state, county, and local court records. Contact details are available on your state archives' website. Contact the National Archives and Records Administration's (NARA) regional facility that serves the state where naturalization occurred to request a search of federal court records.

Post-1906 Naturalizations

After 1906, the courts sent copies of naturalizations to the U.S. Immigration and Naturalization Service (INS). Naturalization records from regional federal courts are held in the nearest NARA's regional facility to the federal court where the naturalization occurred. The National Archives in Washington, DC, hold naturalization records for federal courts in Washington, DC.

The "Non-Immigration" of Enslaved Africans

Enslaved Africans transported across the Atlantic Ocean were not immigrants. Immigration and naturalization documents will not exist for them. Instead, you will need to access slave voyage documents and slave ship manifests held within specialty state and national repositories as well as on online slave ship databases.

There are also ship manifests for enslaved Africans and their enslaved descendants who were transported by ship from the Upper Southern states to the slave-holding states of the Deep South.

You can find more information about slave ship records via:

- African American Heritage Resources, from the U.S. National Archives.
- SlaveVoyages.org, which houses information about slave ships from 1514 to 1866.
- The British National Archives, which features British transatlantic slave trade records.
- Internet searches using the phrase "slave ship manifests."

Citizenship and naturalization are important chapters in an ancestor's life story. Neglecting or not filling in the gaps in this chapter of a person's life can leave significant gaps in their stories. Tracking down these kinds of documents can also lead to remarkable discoveries, like the names of your immigrant ancestor's parents, siblings, or extended family.

With this in mind, let's explore some of the immigration centers for American immigrants in Step 32.

COMPREHEND

STEP 32

Ellis Island and the Multiple Ellis Islands for Enslaved Africans

Ellis Island is the iconic New York harbor island known today as the place where more than 12 million immigrants were processed when they first landed on America's shores. But it's actually had many identities. Purchased by the governors of New Amsterdam from the Mohegan tribe in the 1600s, it had already served as a tavern, a fort, and an ammunition depot long before it became an immigration center. This step covers some of the major events in the island's history. However, one role Ellis Island never played was as a port of entry for enslaved Africans, as you will also learn in this step.

Ellis Island Facts

The following timeline is a quick tour of the major events and changes in the history of Ellis Island. You should consider these highlights if you are searching for immigration records for ancestors who may have passed through Ellis Island's doors.

Ellis Island: A Timeline

1700s

ISLAND ORIGINS

Samuel Ellis was the island's private owner by the 1770s. The island had been called Kioshk, Oyster, Dyre, Bucking, and Anderson's Island.

Over time, Ellis Island morphed from a low, sandy island into a site for pirates, a harbor fort, and an ammunition and ordinance depot named Fort Gibson.

1794–1890
MILITARY PORT TO NATIONAL GATEWAY

Between 1794 and 1890, Ellis Island played a mostly uneventful military role. Following British control of New York Harbor in the Revolutionary War, the newly formed U.S. federal government purchased Ellis Island from New York State in 1808. Ellis Island was approved as a site for fortifications. The fort at Ellis Island was named Fort Gibson in honor of an officer killed during the War of 1812.

1800s
MASS IMMIGRATION

Prior to 1890, the individual states regulated immigration into the United States. Castle Garden in the Battery—originally known as Castle Clinton—served as the New York State immigration station from 1855 to 1890. The new structure on Ellis Island opened on January 1, 1892. Irish immigrant Annie Moore and her two brothers were the first immigrants to be processed at Ellis Island.

1897–1900
FIRE!

In the early morning hours of June 15, 1897, a fire on Ellis Island burned the immigration station to the ground. No lives were lost. However, many years of federal and state immigration records dating back to 1855 went up in flames, along with the wooden buildings that were meant to protect them.

1900
CLASS DIVISION

First- and second-class passengers were not required to undergo the inspection process at Ellis Island. Instead, they had a quick inspection on board their ship. There was a theory that if a person could afford to purchase a first- or second-class ticket, they were less likely to become a public charge in America due to medical or legal reasons.

1907
PEAK IMMIGRATION

Approximately 1.25 million immigrants were processed at Ellis Island!

1924

POST-1924

After 1924, the only people who were detained at Ellis Island were those who had problems with their paperwork as well as war refugees and displaced persons.

1965

NATIONAL MONUMENT

President Lyndon Johnson declared Ellis Island part of the Statue of Liberty National Monument in 1965. The island was opened to the public on a limited basis between 1976 and 1984.

After a $160 million refurbishment, the main building was reopened to the public on September 10, 1990, as the Ellis Island Immigration Museum.

The Many Ellis Islands for Enslaved Africans

The arrival of enslaved Africans in British-held colonial territory is both a simple and complex history. The simple part is that millions of Africans were captured and shipped to America. The complex part is that there was no one place comparable to Ellis Island for the enslaved Africans who were brought to America's shores. While there are manifests for the ships that transported Africans to America, you will not find the Africans listed by name. At best, you will see them grouped by gender and whether they were adults or children. Nor was there a single point of entry. As a result, there is no centralized repository or history center such as Ellis Island containing records documenting the arrival of enslaved Africans.

Hampton (Virginia), Charleston (South Carolina), and New Orleans (Louisiana) were the three main ports that received enslaved Africans. However, much earlier in colonial America's history, Newport (Rhode Island) received more enslaved Africans than any other port in the 13 colonies. Records documenting facts such as these are mostly in private hands, with a fraction available publicly in local, state, or national archives.

The preceding graphic shows the major American ports that served as unofficial Ellis Islands for enslaved Africans. You may find it to be a useful reference as you begin to identify any African ancestors who were brought to the United States before the Civil War.

Understanding the history associated with American ports of entry for immigrants and enslaved Africans can help you in your genealogical research. Knowing how they evolved as immigration centers, the catastrophes that befell them (e.g., fires), and the way they processed arrivals can help you in determining if the records you need to document your ancestors' arrival into the country still exist and where you can find them. This brings us to the next step in researching your immigrant ancestors: searching through and using immigration records.

Slave Ports

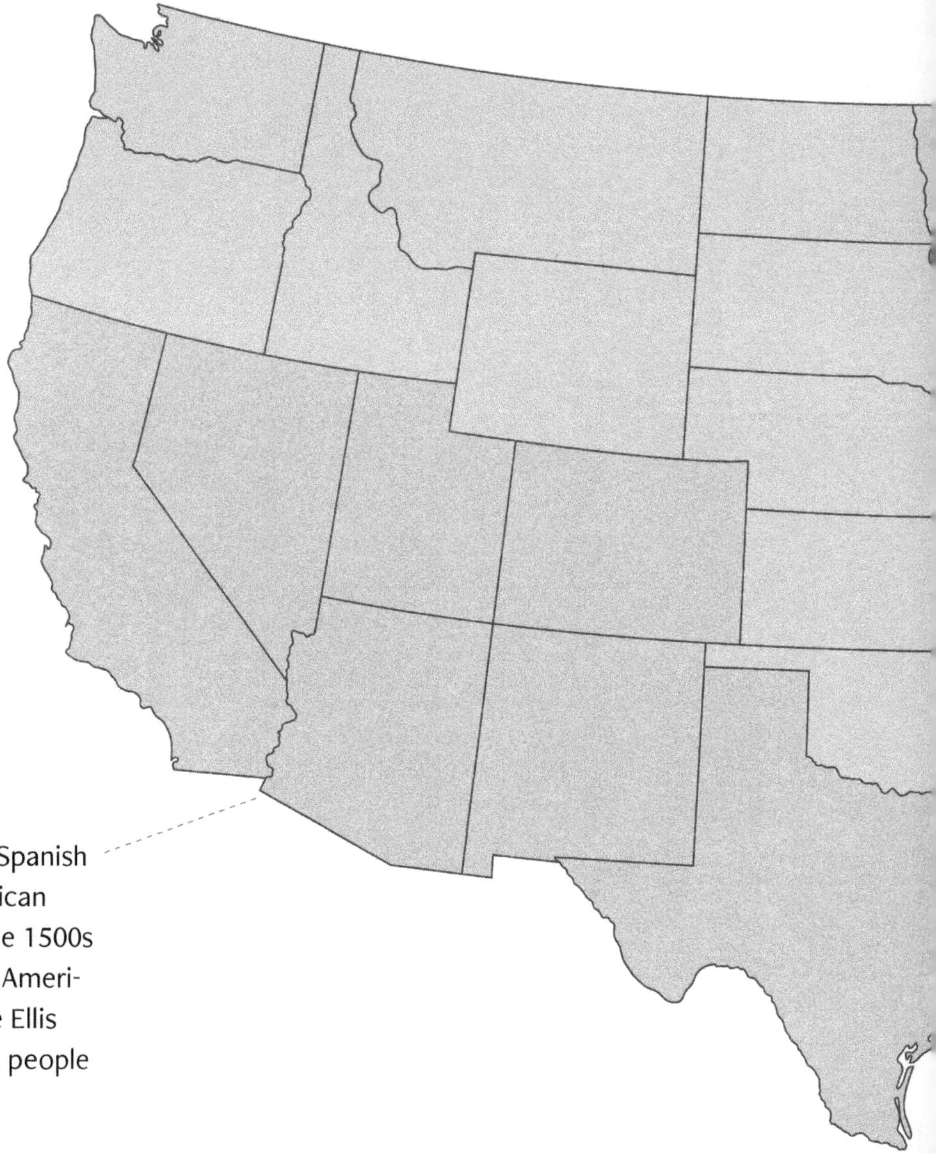

SPANISH-HELD TERRITORIES The Spanish brought Africans and ethnically mixed African Creoles into present-day America from the 1500s until they lost possession of their former American territories. St. Augustine (FL) was the Ellis Island for Africans and African-descended people in Florida.

Importation of enslaved Africans was not widespread in Spanish Texas. However, enslaved Africans were smuggled into Texas between 1816 and 1821 through Galveston Island.

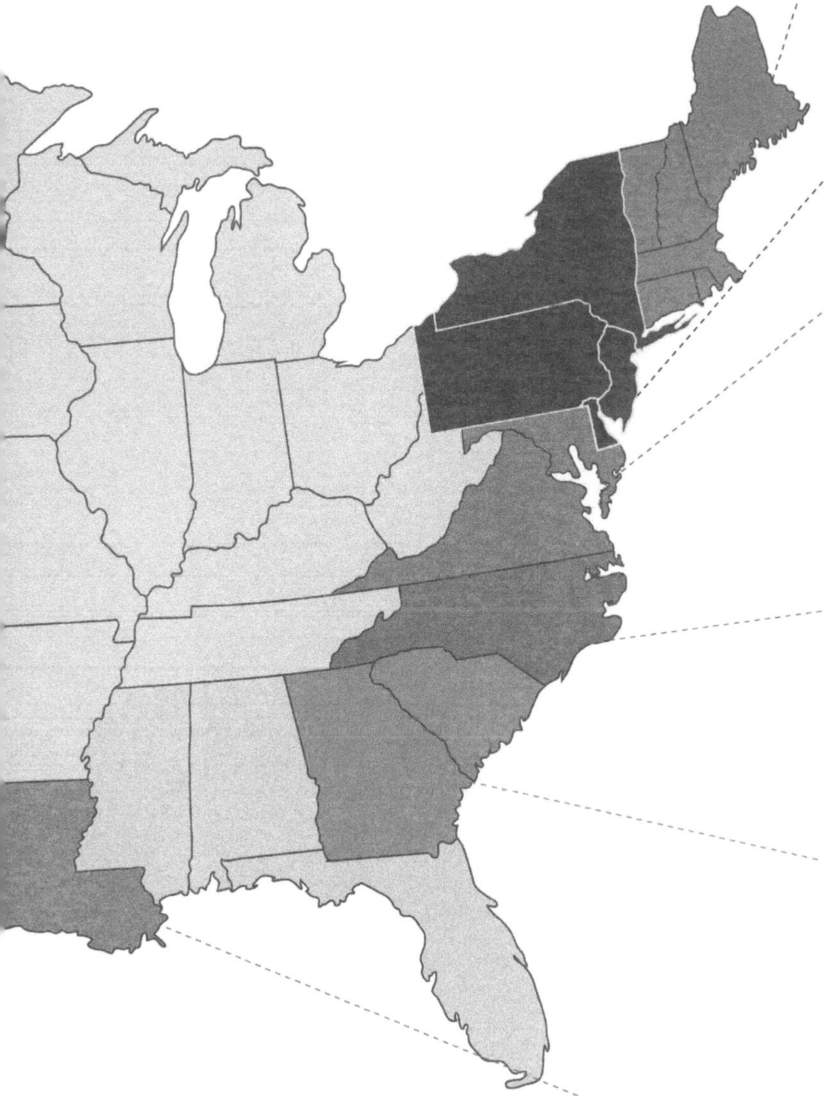

NEW ENGLAND By 1676, Massachusetts merchants started buying slaves in Madagascar and then selling them to Virginians. Massachusetts was the original primary importer of enslaved Africans in New England. Rhode Island ultimately became the biggest slave market in the colonies.

MID-ATLANTIC STATES New York City (NY), Baltimore (MD), and Philadelphia (PA) were the largest slave ports in this region in colonial times.

MARYLAND AND VIRGINIA Annapolis and Baltimore were the largest slave ports in Maryland. Fort Monroe in Hampton (VA) and Norfolk (VA) were two of the Ellis Islands for enslaved Africans in Virginia. The entire Chesapeake region of Virginia witnessed the large-scale importation of enslaved Africans.

NORTH CAROLINA The port at Wilmington was used extensively in the delivery of slaves to the Lower Cape Fear region. Many enslavers in North Carolina purchased enslaved Africans via land routes from South Carolina, Georgia, and the Chesapeake region of Virginia.

SOUTH CAROLINA AND GEORGIA
Sullivan's Island, a tiny quarantine station in Charleston harbor, was the main Ellis Island of black America. Many of the early settlers of what would become South Carolina arrived from the island of Barbados, bringing hundreds of enslaved Africans with them. Savannah would become a major slave port in the eighteenth century.

LOUISIANA New Orleans was the Ellis Island for enslaved Africans brought into Louisiana.

STEP 33

Search and Use Naturalization Records

Not every immigrant who arrived in the United States became a naturalized citizen, and there will not be any naturalization records for these people. However, for those who did apply for citizenship, naturalization records can provide a gold mine of information that will answer many of our 5 Ws questions.

Naturalization Records

Claire Prechtel-Kluskens' article "The Location of Naturalization Records" forms the basis for this step.

An alien could file for naturalization in any court of record from 1790 through much of the twentieth century. (As mentioned earlier, a court of record is a trial court or appellate court in which a record of the proceedings is captured and preserved for the possibility of appeal.) An applicant would typically visit a court near where they lived. But other courts handled naturalization applications as well, including county supreme, circuit, district, equity, chancery, probate, and common pleas courts. Some state supreme courts also naturalized aliens, including those in Indiana, Idaho, Iowa, Maine, New Jersey, and South Dakota. Federal court, such as U.S. district courts or circuit courts, in large cities also handled the naturalization process.

The Two-Step Naturalization Process

From its inception by Congress in 1790, naturalization was generally a two-step process that took a minimum of five years to complete (known as the "Five-Year Rule").

After a two-year residency within the United States, the first step would be for an alien to file a "declaration of intent" (also known as "first papers") to become a citizen.

After an additional three years, the second step would be for an alien to file a petition for naturalization. A certificate of citizenship was issued to the applicant once the petition was granted. It wasn't necessary for these two steps to take place in the same court or in the same state.

Generally speaking, a declaration of intent contains more genealogically useful information than the petition. The declaration may include the alien's month and year (or possibly date) of immigration into the United States.

There are a few exceptions to the Five-Year Rule. The first involves the wives and children of naturalized men. From 1790 to 1922, "derivative citizenship" was granted to wives and minor children of naturalized men, meaning they automatically became citizens.

1 Children under the age of 21 automatically became naturalized citizens through derivative citizenship from 1790 to 1940.

2 An 1862 law allowed honorably discharged Army veterans of any war to petition for naturalization without previously having filed a declaration of intent after only one year of residence in the United States. An 1894 law extended the same privilege to honorably discharged five-year veterans of the Navy or Marine Corps.

Knowledge about an immigrant ancestor's war service may help you in identifying when and where your ancestor may have started the naturalization process.

Additional Documents

Naturalization depositions: Witnesses were required for the naturalization hearing process. Their statements at a hearing may contain family history information.

Certificate of arrival: Immigrants had to prove to a court that they had legally entered the United States from 1906 onward. They proved this by using a "certificate of arrival" issued by the Immigration and Naturalization Service. This certificate noted the name of the port where the alien arrived, their arrival date, and the name of the ship they had sailed on.

Alien registration files: The Alien Registration Act of 1940 required noncitizens living in the United States, age 14 and older, to register. Each registered alien was assigned an Alien Registration Number (A-number). The registration form, part of the immigrant's Alien File (A-file), contains a wide range of details, including all names a person used, their date and place of birth, immigration date, the name of the ship they arrived aboard, activities and organization affiliations, and criminal history.

States with Donated Naturalization Records in the National Archives, Washington, DC

Following is a list of states that have donated their naturalization records to the United States National Archives:

* California
* Connecticut
* Illinois
* Indiana
* Iowa
* Maine
* Massachusetts
* New Hampshire
* New York
* Rhode Island
* Vermont
* Washington State
* Wisconsin

Search Strategies

When researching an immigrant ancestor, pay particular attention to:

- How a surname may have changed from its original spelling.
- How different parts of the naturalization process might be filed in different courts in the various places an ancestor lived. You may be required to check several sites and sources.

Census records can provide numerous clues that may help you in your research:

- 1820, 1830, 1840, and 1870 censuses contain a question asking if a person was an alien or a citizen.
- 1900, 1910, 1920, and 1930 censuses ask the year an immigrant arrived in the United States and if a noncitizen had begun or completed naturalization.
- The 1920 census asked the year the individual was naturalized.

Tracking Down Naturalization Documents

There are no hard-and-fast rules about where you can find naturalization-related documents. However, there are some basic considerations to guide you in your search.

County court–held naturalization records may still be available at the county court, in a county or state archive, or in a regional archive. It is not unusual for county court employees to say that their naturalization records are at the National Archives or that their court never conducted naturalizations. Generally speaking, however, the National Archives does not have naturalization records created in state or local courts. It is up to you to determine the current location of the naturalization records you are looking for.

Look for the "Naturalization Records" section of the National Archives website.

Don't forget to update your research log and timelines with all the discoveries you make while investigating your ancestors' immigration records.

One special set of immigration records that are packed with useful genealogical information is ship passenger logs. We will explore researching passenger logs in Step 34.

STEP 34

Find and Review Passenger Ship Logs

Passenger ship logs are a rich source of information about your ancestors. While not always easy to locate, these logs are worth the effort. What job did your immigrant fourth great-grandparents have back in their native Palermo, Italy? How old were they when they arrived? Did your third great-grandmother Janie arrive in Baltimore on her own or with her parents and siblings? Passenger ship logs just might have the answers.

These logs, also known as immigration records, can provide you with information such as:

- Your ancestor's nationality, place of birth, and last place of residence.
- The date your ancestor entered the United States and their destination.
- Your ancestor's occupation, age, sex, height, and eye and hair color.
- The ship's name, master, and ports of departure and arrival.
- Family members or others who traveled on the same ship as well as their ages and places of birth.
- Names and addresses of relatives your immigrant ancestor was joining in the United States.
- The amount of money and other items your ancestors brought with them.

Where Were Ship Manifests Stored?

Before 1820, ship manifests were typically filed at the port of arrival; they were not stored in a central depository. Because they were not centralized, many manifests have been destroyed or lost. Those that have survived are scattered among numerous libraries, museums, historical and genealogical societies, and private family archives. However, many passenger lists for this time period have been extracted and published in books, journals, CDs, microfilm, and websites and databases.

Getting Started

The best place to begin searching for an immigrant's entry is the port closest to where the person was living when they first appear in official records (such as a census). These documents may include information about the country of an ancestor's birth, when they arrived in the United States, and their naturalization status.

A Helpful Hint

If your ancestor had relatives who arrived in the United States before their arrival, try to locate immigration records for these family member(s) to see if your ancestor lived with or near them. These records may shed some light on where and when your ancestor arrived.

Current Locations for Passenger Lists

There are several places to check for ship passenger lists.

- The National Archives
    - Microfilm housed in the archives includes passenger list indexes for ships arriving at the Port of New York for the years 1820–1846 and 1897–1943.
- Access to Archival Databases (AAD)
    - Data files covering Russian arrivals to the United States (1834–1897)
    - Records for passengers who arrived at the Port of New York during the Irish Famine (January 12, 1846–December 31, 1851)
    - Data files covering German immigration to the United States (1850–1897)
    - Data files covering Italian immigration to the United States (1855–1900)
- Castle Garden Immigration Center
    - A free online searchable database created by the Battery Conservancy. It hosts 10 million immigrant entries for the years 1830 to 1892 (the year Ellis Island opened).
- Church of Jesus Christ of Latter-Day Saints' Family History Centers
- Ancestry.com

- Town, county, and state archives
- Historical and genealogical societies (including libraries)

Search for online resources and databases with information on passenger ship logs by typing the search string "Finding and Using Passenger Records & Ship Information" into your preferred search engine.

Passenger lists may take some time and effort to locate and access. However, they are worth the effort to track down because of the wealth of information they contain. You might even find some extended family members—like your ancestors' aunts, uncles, and cousins—in the process.

What should you do if you can't find immigration, naturalization, or passenger log records? We'll explore that in Step 35.

STEP 35

Track Down Elusive Arrival and Naturalization Records

Naturalization records have become easier to find and access, with millions now digitized and available online. However, there's still a chance you'll run into trouble tracking down your ancestor's arrival and immigration records. Never fear—this step is designed to help you overcome these barriers and find those elusive records.

Remember, not all immigrants applied for citizenship. For these ancestors, you may be able to locate arrival records, but there won't be any naturalization files or documents.

Location, Location, Location

Before you can break through this particular brick wall, you will need to determine where your ancestor lived in the United States. This is a topic we've explored in previous steps. Once you know where your ancestor lived, you're more likely to be able to find where they filed their naturalization paperwork.

Research Resources

Resources for tracking down immigration and naturalization records—including whether or not your ancestor became a U.S. citizen—are listed below.

U.S. Federal Censuses

Notations about whether a person was naturalized or not can be found on federal censuses in 1870 and from 1900 to 1940. The 1920 census also notes the year the person was naturalized and whether the following were filed in court: a declaration of intention, a petition for naturalization, depositions, and a copy of the certificate of naturalization.

Census-takers also used abbreviations to designate citizenship status, which offer a wealth of information for genealogical research. These include AL (Alien), NA (Naturalized), NR (Not Reported [not given]), PA (First Papers filed), IN (Declaration of Intention), and Am Cit (American Citizen born abroad).

Passport Applications

When applying for a passport, a naturalized citizen noted his or her year of naturalization. Passport records can be found on Ancestry.com, Fold3, and FamilySearch.org.

Voter Registration Records

An immigrant had to be a citizen to vote after 1906. Check your county or city repositories, local libraries, and historical and genealogical societies for voter registration records. Availability varies by location.

Land Records

A declaration of intention had to be filed before an immigrant could apply for land under the Homestead Act of 1862. After this, an immigrant had to wait for five years to secure the patent to the homestead. Some homestead applications contain copies of naturalization records.

You can obtain land record files from the National Archives, a courthouse of record, or the Bureau of Land Management office in the state where your immigrant ancestor secured their land.

Military Records

Aliens who served in the U.S. Army after 1862 and were honorably discharged could apply for citizenship on an abbreviated timeline. This was not a guarantee of citizenship. Military service records are not likely to have copies of an ancestor's naturalization record. However, if the veteran applied for a pension, you may locate such documentation there.

World War I draft records indicate naturalization status and can be found on Ancestry.com, Fold3, and FamilySearch.org.

Female Immigrant Ancestors

Women rarely applied for naturalization before 1922. They became citizens when their husbands became naturalized. A foreign-born woman who married a U.S. citizen could forego the declaration of intention before 1922 and just file a petition for naturalization. However, if a foreign woman married a foreign man in the United States, she would be required to start her naturalization proceedings with a declaration of intention.

Tracking down elusive arrival and naturalization records can be a challenge, but using the information and resources provided in this step should increase your chances of success.

If you're still struggling to find immigration-related records, revisit Step 23: The Most Common Brick Walls in Research (page 73) and follow the suggestions. You can also send an email or letter of inquiry—which just happens to be the subject we'll be covering in Step 36.

Offline Resources

If your online search doesn't yield any results, you may need to check microfilm records for the court(s) where you believe your ancestor may have filed for naturalization. You can visit the courthouse or send a written request. Remember, county courts and state supreme courts are the most common locations for naturalization filings. Do keep in mind that an ancestor could have also filed at a circuit, district, probate, federal, or common pleas court. *The Red Book: American State, County, and Town Sources* offers summaries of court records available in every state.

It might be helpful to check the courthouse's website or call ahead before you visit to ask about locations of historical records and research rules.

STEP 36

Write a Successful Record Request

At some point in your genealogical research, you will need to write a letter or email requesting certain records. A succinct, fact-rich inquiry can make the difference between receiving a reply or not.

Keep It Short

There's no need to include your family history or a lengthy explanation of why you are doing research when approaching an individual or an organization for information about an ancestor. You're more likely to receive a response to a short, concise email or letter.

This is especially essential when requesting copies of vital records. Clerks working in such offices receive numerous requests every day, and they don't have time to read a long email or letter.

Be Specific

- Explain exactly what you are looking for.
- Provide as much specific, relevant information as possible about the ancestor you are researching.

Points to Consider in Your Request

- If possible, include the exact or approximate date on which the event you are researching took place.
- State your relationship to the person about whom you are seeking information. Public institutions can only provide copies of certain types of documents to immediate relatives.
- Call ahead to find out if research or copying fees will be charged and, if so, the organization's preferred payment method. Then enclose any money with your request.

- Make sure the correspondence you send is straightforward, easy to understand, and free of errors. Also, double-check that the names and dates you have included are accurate.
- Enclose a self-addressed stamped envelope.
- Say "thank you." It is always polite to thank someone for their time and effort on your behalf. Let the person who receives your letter know that you appreciate their help.

Keep a copy of each request you send in your research log. Note the following:

- The date on which you made the request
- The name and address of the person or institution
- The type of information requested
- The type of information received
- Any money that you sent along with the request

Generally speaking, staff who work in the public sector and handle genealogy-related materials are happy to help you find the documents and records that you need. However, before they can help you, you must help them by providing record requests that are clear and focused.

One example of an information request you might draft is inquiring about an old published family history book, which is a subject we will explore in Step 37.

Facts to Include in Your Information Request

Genealogy.com suggests including as many of the following as possible in your email or letter:

- The full name of the person you are researching (with a maiden name, for female ancestors)
- Date and place of birth
- Father's, mother's, husband's, and wife's first names and surnames
- Date of marriage (if you are looking for record of a marriage or divorce, include the names of both spouses)
- Place of marriage or divorce
- Date and place of death
- Date of immigration
- Religion (if applicable, particularly if writing to a religious organization)

STEP 37

Search for Published Family Histories

Family history books are superb resources for researching ancestral families. In their pages, you can find riveting stories and forgotten family events. You may even discover old ancestral pictures you will likely have never seen. Great family history books can also give you an idea of family traits and eccentricities.

You will need to do your due diligence when using family history books. Ask others for their opinion about the accuracy of information in the book you are reading. However, while some family history books might suffer from inaccurate genealogical information, they can still provide glimpses into the prevailing social attitudes and customs that influenced our ancestors' lives. This type of book can supply a personal perspective and intimate details that are not readily available elsewhere.

There are numerous places where you can find published family history books.

Seven Places to Get You Started

1 Local research librarians

Your local or state research librarians can advise you on the family history books in their collection and point you to other places where you can find such books.

See Step 28: Identify Community Support (page 91)

2 State archives

State archives, including university archives in the colony or state(s) where your ancestor lived, may also contain copies of family history books.

3 Local and regional historical and genealogical societies

Historical and genealogical societies can advise you on the family history books in their collection as well as point you to other resources that may carry them.

See Step 28: Identify Community Support (page 91)

4 Library of Congress

The Library of Congress has a vast collection of family history books. You can search its website to find books and other materials that feature your family. Some family history books may only be available on microfilm.

5 Daughters of the American Revolution (DAR) and Sons of the American Revolution (SAR) research libraries

The national headquarters of the DAR (Washington, DC) and SAR (Louisville, Kentucky) have family history and lineage books for qualifying patriot ancestors. Some chapters may also have family history books.

6 The Church of Jesus Christ of Latter-Day Saints' Family History Centers

The Church of Jesus Christ of Latter-Day Saints has Family History Centers throughout the world. You can search its website for the titles that these centers hold. Some family history books may only be available on microfilm.

7 Internet

Try using some simple Internet search strings to see if free versions of family history books are available for you to access online. Examples of search strings are "Jones family of Virginia lineage," "Jones family of Virginia pedigree," "Jones family of Virginia lineage book," and "Jones family of Virginia pedigree book."

Internet Archive, Google Books, and FamilySearch host free, downloadable family history books.

Reading family history books can be an exciting part of your family history research. This type of book will take you beyond names and dates to starting to explore the stories of your ancestors' lives.

STEP 38

Listen to the Music of Your Heritage

Music is an excellent way to connect with your cultural heritage. Whether you've discovered an ancestral connection to Irish Céilí, Khoisan Folk, Indian Ragas, Jewish Klezmer, African American work songs, Tuvan throat music, or old English Pastoral music—you can discover every kind of music online as well as in person at local specialty music stores.

Exploring your musical heritage is a powerful, affirming, and enjoyable way to feel a connection with those who came before us. It's also something that's fun to share with the family to get them interested in your research. Music is something that most people can relate to and connect with.

Popular online streaming music providers that feature music from around the globe are listed in the following chart.

Music App/ Streaming Service	Website URL
Amazon Music	music.amazon.com
Apple Music	www.apple.com/ apple-music/
Deezer	www.deezer.com
NetEase (Asia)	music.163.com
Pandora	www.pandora.com
SoundCloud	www.soundcloud.com
Spotify	www.spotify.com
TuneIn	www.tunein.com
YouTube	music.youtube.com

STEP 39

Searching for Orphaned, Adopted, and Bound-Out Children

Orphaned and adopted children, as well as children who were apprenticed or "bound out," present a unique research challenge. Family-related information, one of the richest veins of genealogical data, is often missing. However, it is not impossible to track down some clues about ancestors who were separated from their birth families in childhood, and this step offers resources and strategies for doing so.

Between 1854 and 1929, cities along America's eastern coast faced a growing crisis in the number of orphaned, abandoned, and homeless children. During this time, nearly 200,000 children were removed from these cities and placed with families in the mostly rural areas in the Midwest. This large-scale transportation of children is known as the Orphan Train Movement.

Orphan Trains

In the mid-1850s, three New York–based charitable institutions (the Children's Aid Society, the Children's Village, and the New York Foundling Hospital) spearheaded what came to be known as the Orphan Train Movement. Through this program, thousands of orphaned and homeless children were placed on trains and sent to live with foster families, mostly in the Midwest. Orphan trains were sent to 45 states as well as Canada and Mexico. In the early years, Indiana received the largest number of children from orphan trains out of any state in the United States.

To give you an idea of the scale, the Children's Aid Society averaged 3,000 children per train between 1855 and 1875.

The program ended in the 1920s, with the beginning of organized foster care.

If you believe your ancestor may have been an orphan or otherwise parentless during this time period, you may want to research orphan trains. This is particularly true if the person lived in a city in New England or the mid-Atlantic states and seemingly disappeared from official records in the place where they were born.

Look for an archive of orphan train children's stories maintained by the Orphan Train Heritage Society and for other records of these children kept by the National Orphan Train Museum in Concordia, Kansas.

Adopted Ancestors

A Short History of Adoption in the United States

Early Colonial Period

17TH AND EARLY 18TH CENTURIES

The British instituted a policy of rounding up orphaned, abandoned, and homeless children and shipping them to the American colonies. These children were apprentices or indentured servants. Most were settled in the colonies to the south of New England

Mid- to Late Colonial Period

BOUND OUT

Orphaned children or children born to poor parents who could not adequately provide for them were "bound out" and apprenticed.

An Informal Process

Prior to 1851, adoption legislation did not exist. Adoptions, as we think of them, were informal. Orphaned or abandoned children could find a new home with a relative or a neighbor. Alternatively, the local parish elders and community leaders would apprentice such children so that they could learn a trade that would provide for them when they reached adulthood.

The First State Legislation

1851 AND 1898

Massachusetts was the first state to introduce adoption laws (the Massachusetts Adoption of Children Act of 1851). The New York State Charities Aid Association, the first specialized child-placement program, was organized in 1898.

United States Children's Bureau

1912

Congress created the United States Children's Bureau in the Department of Labor in 1912 "to investigate and report on all matters pertaining to the welfare of children and child life among all classes of our people."

An Official Process

1970s

While policies and procedures differed from state to state, basic adoption policies became regulated in the 1970s. From then onward, adoptions have been largely handled by thousands of adoption agencies. Inconsistent adoption practices and policies means there isn't consistency between the adoption records used, how they were stored or maintained, and whether such files are open to the public or closed/sealed.

Records of "Illegitimate" Births

An illegitimate child is a child whose parents were not married at the time of his or her birth. Other terms you see for these children include "natural-born," "bastard," and "base-born." Less common terms you may come across are "spurious," "imputed," "reputed," and "misbegotten."

"Bastardy bonds" were a tool used by parishes to protect the government (originally the British Crown and, after the Revolution, the early states) from being financially liable for children born out of wedlock. The bond placed the burden of supporting a child on the father if the child's mother became unable to support or provide for the child.

The Bastardy Bond Process

The process began with a public complaint that an unwed woman was pregnant. The parish elders then issued a warrant, and the woman was brought into court.

The mother was questioned under oath, where she was asked to name the child's father. If she identified the father, an additional warrant was issued to bring the father before the local justices of the peace.

The father posted a bond to appear in court and answer charges. If the father was found guilty, he would then have to post a bond for support of the child. This document was the bastardy bond.

If the woman refused to name the father, she, her father, or some other interested party would post the bond. Failure to name the father or to post a bond could mean a jail sentence for the mother. North Carolina and Virginia regularly used bastardy bonds. To see if bastardy bonds were used in your state's history and which counties kept these records, search for the keywords "[State and/or county name] bastardy bonds."

Additional Records That May Indicate Illegitimacy

- Birth and Death Records: Some birth records list the mother as well as a note that the child was "illegitimate." Generally, the father's name would not be included in the birth record of an illegitimate child.
- Quaker Records: One or both parents could be disowned, or cast out, from their Quaker community for having an illegitimate child, and Quaker records are especially forthcoming about the topic. The women's monthly minutes are an excellent place to find this information. These were monthly summaries of community-related topics, issues, events, and occurrences that Quaker women wrote about their local religious community.
- Court Records: Children's records can be found in the FamilySearch Catalog under minute books, civil action papers, miscellaneous, bastardy bonds, apprenticeship, orphan, probate, and guardianship records.
- Apprentice Records: These records varied by location. In some cases, they list the names of the child's parents or guardians. If only the mother is listed as the child's named parent, then he or she may have been born out of wedlock. Try a keyword search of "apprentice" or "apprenticeship" plus the state you are researching to access information about apprenticeship papers.
- Guardianship Records: Family members were sometimes appointed to be a child's guardian. This information will be included in county guardianship records. However, these records may not clearly state if a child was illegitimate.

"Bound-Out" Children

During the early colonial period and most of the 1800s, orphans and children from families that were too poor to care for them were apprenticed or "bound out" to learn a trade. In some instances, families made this decision, but often the action was taken by parish elders, a court, or an overseer of the poor. Typically, boys were bound out to learn a trade or farming. Girls were usually bound out for domestic servitude. Binding-out records can typically be found in local and state archives.

9 Details You Can Learn from a Binding Order

1 The name of the apprentice's parents or guardian.

2 Where they lived when they were bound out and during their apprenticeship.

3 The name of the apprentice's master and mistress.

4 The trade the apprentice will learn.

5 The number of years the apprentice will serve.

6 The provisions or services that the master or mistress guarantees to provide.

7 The rules by which the apprentice must abide.

8 Schooling provisions, if any.

9 What, if anything, the apprentice would receive from the master or mistress upon completion of his or her term of service.

Finding information about orphaned, adopted, and bound-out children is not easy. Information documenting them in a family context is usually missing. You may have the name of their mother but not their father, or you may not have either parent's name. However, armed with the information you have learned through this and the preceding steps, you can create a research strategy that chips away at the unknown aspects of their lives and discover what you need to find their place within your family.

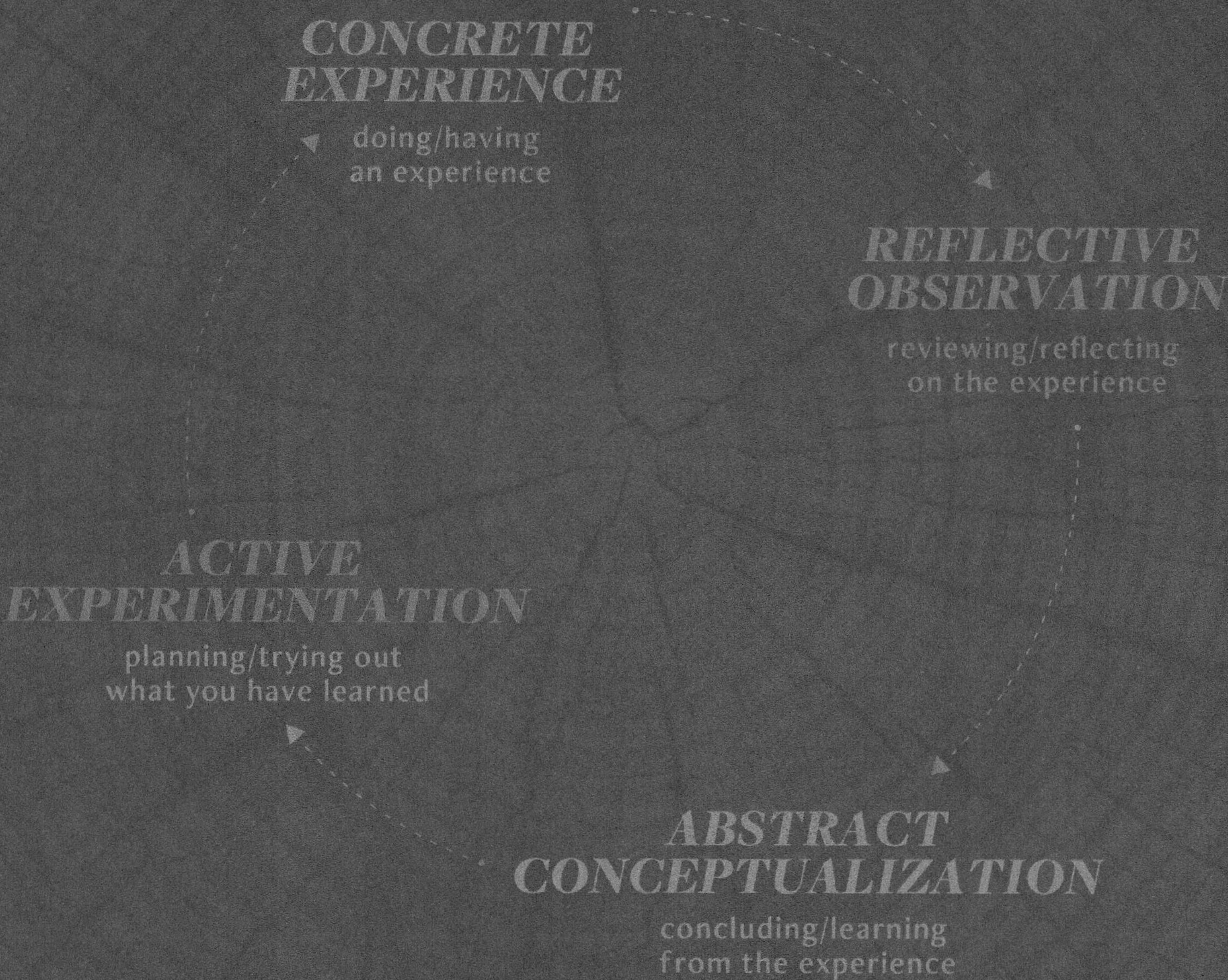
CONCRETE EXPERIENCE
doing/having an experience
REFLECTIVE OBSERVATION
reviewing/reflecting on the experience
ABSTRACT CONCEPTUALIZATION
concluding/learning from the experience
ACTIVE EXPERIMENTATION
planning/trying out what you have learned

STEP 40

Reflect

REFLECT

Take some time to reflect on the new skills and information we have covered.

Check in with yourself by answering the following questions:

- How well do you understand exploring your heritage and ethnicity?
- Are you able to identify sources of information and sources of local research support?
- Do you feel confident about developing approaches to researching your immigrant ancestors?
- How confident are you that you can develop approaches for brick-wall ancestors?

Give yourself permission to acknowledge if you are still unclear about a topic that we have explored together. Reread a previous step, if you need to. Remember, genealogy is an endurance activity, not a sprint.

Make sure you really understand and can apply the fundamental concepts you have explored up to this point. You will need to understand them before we continue to explore different aspects of genealogy research, beginning with Step 41, which explores migration routes.

COMPREHEND

STEP 41

The Importance of Migration Routes

The story of America is the story of the large-scale movement of people. It's a story of people who chose to migrate to new areas of the expanding country to farm more productive land, find new business opportunities, or look for a fresh start.

This step explores a handful of the major migration routes; however, there were hundreds of migratory routes that people traveled across the country from the early colonial period throughout the nineteenth century.

To discover more of the routes your ancestors may have used, enter the following search string into your preferred search engine: "American settler migration routes."

Pioneer and Settler Migration Routes

The Wilderness Road

The famous American pioneer Daniel Boone established the Wilderness Road in the early 1770s as a westward path into Kentucky. Thousands of settlers used this road from the late 1700s through the early 1800s. The road passed through the Cumberland Gap, a natural opening in the Appalachian mountain range near the junction of Kentucky, Virginia, and Tennessee. In its time, the Wilderness Road became one of the main pathways westward.

The National Road

When Ohio became a state in 1803, there was no road to connect it to the surrounding states. The National Road was built to meet this need, with construction beginning in western Maryland in 1811. Later, it became the first federal roadway in America, making it possible to travel from Indiana to Washington, DC.

The Erie Canal

The Erie Canal, one of the most significant engineering projects of its day, was hailed as a marvel when it opened in 1825.

The canal connected the Great Lakes to the Hudson River and New York City. It carried thousands of settlers westward at its height during the first half of the nineteenth century.

The Oregon Trail

In the 1840s, the Oregon Trail was the way westward for thousands of settlers. Starting in Independence, Missouri, it stretched for 2,000 miles, terminating in the Willamette Valley of Oregon.

The Santa Fe Trail

Started in 1821, the Santa Fe Trail was a route built through central North America. It connected Franklin, Missouri, to Santa Fe, New Mexico.

The Old Spanish Trail

The Old Spanish Trail existed for a brief time between 1830 and 1848. Its primary function was as a trade route linking Santa Fe, New Mexico, to Los Angeles, California. The trail was composed of two courses: the South or Main Branch, which headed northwest past Colorado's San Juan Mountains and terminated near Green River, Utah; and the North Branch, which went north into Colorado's San Luis Valley before crossing westward.

Major Forced Migrations

Trail of Tears (Native American)

The Trail of Tears was a series of forced Native Americans removals. The exodus began from their ancestral homelands in the southeastern United States to areas that lay to the west of the Mississippi River that had been designated as Indian Territory. President Andrew Jackson signed the Indian Removal Act in 1830. By 1840, tens of thousands of Native Americans were removed from the southeastern states and forced to move across the Mississippi to Indian Territory, which is mostly now in the state of Oklahoma.

The 5,043-mile-long Trail of Tears covers nine states: Alabama, Arkansas, Georgia, Illinois, Kentucky, Missouri, North Carolina, Oklahoma, and Tennessee.

The Second Middle Passage (African American)

The Second Middle Passage was the term for the mass relocation of enslaved African Americans in the early to mid-nineteenth century. More than a million enslaved people were taken in a forced migration from the Upper South (Maryland, Delaware, Virginia, Tennessee, Kentucky, North Carolina, South Carolina, and the District of Columbia) to the territories and newly admitted states of the Lower South and the Western Territories (Georgia, Alabama, Florida, Louisiana, Mississippi, Arkansas, and Texas).

The Great Migration

Between 1916 and 1970, six million African Americans moved from the Southern states to states in the Northeast, Midwest, and West as part of the Great Migration (also referred to as the Great Northward Migration). Baltimore, Boston, Chicago, Denver, Detroit, Los Angeles, New York City, Oakland, Philadelphia, Phoenix, Pittsburg, Portland, San Francisco, St. Louis, Seattle, and Washington, DC, were among the places where Southern African Americans settled during this period.

Migrating across America was no easy feat. Families who moved into the new territories that were opening up left everything they knew behind, including their families in some cases. Uncovering the stories of a family's fight against the odds or just learning about the ordeals these families faced will make you look at your ancestors in an entirely new light.

You may be able to gain some additional insights into why your ancestors participated in non-forced migrations as well. These may come from financial records. Did your ancestor's household increase or decrease in number after a migration? Did your ancestors prosper in the new town they moved to? Chances are financial records can help you answer those questions. We will explore the benefits of working with financial records in Step 42.

STEP 42

Understand Ancestral Financial Records

Financial records may not sound like the most exciting records to research, but these records can be packed with useful information. Tax lists, for instance, document your ancestor's presence in a specific place at a particular date. They also tell you if an ancestor owned property and, if so, how that property was used. These lists can also reveal:

- A person's occupation
- A description of the property that was taxed
- A list of the person's personal property
- The number of taxable males in the household
- The number of minor children
- The number of enslaved people within a household

Telling a Story with Financial Records

Tax lists are also important in genealogical research because they can reveal changes in an ancestor's circumstances. An increase in the amount of property and possessions an ancestor owned paints a picture of increasing prosperity. On the other hand, tax records showing a decreasing amount of property and possessions depicts a story of financial hardship and struggle.

Tax documents can also tell us about an ancestor's age. Heads of households did not pay taxes on males under the age of 16. Older men between 50 and 60 years old were not taxable, as they were considered to have "aged out" of paying tax. Exceptions were made in some areas for veterans, ministers, and those deemed "paupers" (those too poor to pay the tax).

The age when men's names appeared on some types of tax lists was determined by law—16, 18, and 21 were popular ages—and usually meant these "single freemen" (as they were called in some jurisdictions) had to pay the head tax even if they didn't own land or significant personal property. It's not unusual for these men to begin to be listed two or three years later than their ages would justify—attracting the tax collector's eye was no more popular in the past than today. Using these lists, you can trace family units that lack children's birth records.

Young men often graduated to owing a tax on personal property when they married and gained control of their wife's dowry from their father-in-law. Women, however, are not commonly found on historical tax lists because of their unequal status under the law. About the only exceptions were when widows were granted use of or income from land after their husbands died.

Tax records can reveal the financial history of an ancestor from young adulthood to old age. You can follow the tale of an ancestor who began life as an apprentice, his marriage, the number of children he had, his occupation, the first piece of land he bought, and the establishment of his business through to the dispersal of his property after his death.

Newspapers can also be used to research an ancestor's finances. Business advertisements, articles about an ancestor's business or business affairs, and bankruptcies are all useful sources of information.

Writer Judy G. Russell's website The Legal Genealogist provides excellent guidance on how to pull the most information you can from tax lists and other taxation documents.

Think about an ancestor's financial records over different periods of time as though they were chapters in a book. They move a story forward, backward, and even sideways. The story you uncover could be about financial hardship, an overnight success, modest prosperity, or so much more. For more details on the very last chapter of your ancestor's life, consider researching coroner's records and obituaries—a topic we will cover in Step 43.

A Quick Overview of Taxes in the United States

COVERAGE: Americans have paid local and county taxes since early colonial times. State and federal taxation began when the colonies became a country. Income taxes were instituted in the twentieth century, and access to these records is covered by strict privacy rules.

TAX DEBT: A typical penalty is a fine for failure to pay a tax. County courts could, and did, order tax debtors to work off the debt by working for the county. If there is a history of repeated tax debts and your ancestor suddenly disappears from a county's tax records, he or she may have moved elsewhere to start anew.

STORAGE: Record locations generally follow the type of government levying the tax:

* Towns or municipalities keep city and town tax records. Colonial-era taxes are referred to as a poll, tithable, or head tax.
* Courthouse or county archives hold county tax records.
* State taxes are stored in state archives.
* Business licenses records, professional fees, and licenses are kept by courthouses, county archives, and state archives. These will have limited personal information.
* Inheritance or estate taxes are held by state archives.
* The National Archives store federal tax records.

FEDERAL TAXES: Federal taxes were inconsistently levied until the first income tax of 1913. The 1798 United States Direct Tax, nicknamed the Window Tax (the valuation of homes was based in part on the number of windows), is recognized as the first federal tax. Window Tax returns contain information about the number of acres in the property, construction materials, and structure sizes.

DETAILS: Tax records will usually include:

* The names of individual taxpayers.
* A description of land or personal property being taxed.
* Neighbors' names and property.
* Changes in property ownership.
* Estimated birth dates for single men.

To conduct an online search for your ancestor's tax records, use the name of the government unit issuing the tax (such as Virginia) as your search string plus "tax lists," "tax records," or "taxation."

STEP 43

Review Coroner's Records and Obituaries

English common law required that coroners in the American colonies investigate suspicious deaths. You can find records of their investigations from as early as the 1600s. Starting in the nineteenth century, medical examiners replaced coroners in some localities.

Coroners are public officials whose primary purpose is to investigate deaths believed to have been caused by unnatural causes or circumstances. A coroner's inquest is the process used to determine whether a death was from natural or unnatural causes.

Coroners investigated all unexplained deaths from drownings, mishaps, and murders—they even investigated cases of suspected death by witchcraft. As is the case today, not every death warranted investigation by a coroner. However, you might find coroner's records for ancestors who perished in accidents, suicides, or crimes. (Local history books are an excellent source for information on these kinds of incidents!)

The role of an obituary, on the other hand, is to inform a community that someone has died.

Coroner's Records

U.S. coroner's records are available online and offline. They are maintained by local morgues, state archives, or local historical societies.

Coroner's records are confidential and are disclosed at the coroner's discretion. Some coroner's offices will not release records without proof of a relationship to the deceased and a statement indicating how the information in the record will be used.

Coroner's reports usually contain the following information:

- Name, age, address, sex, and race of the deceased
- Location where the body was found and, if different, the location where the death occurred
- Name of the person reporting the death
- Name of the person certifying the death
- Date and location of an autopsy
- Name of the person who performed the autopsy
- Probable cause, probable manner, and probable mechanism of death

Coroner's reports, mortality schedules, and death certificates can reveal diseases or health conditions your family is prone to, such as heart disease or vitamin deficiencies. This information is a key reason why you should record a cause of death in your research log.

To search for coroner's records online, try using the following search string: "[county] [state] coroner's records OR coroner's inquests." For example, "Henrico County Virginia coroner's records" or "Edgefield County South Carolina coroner's inquest."

Another often-overlooked death record is the mortality schedule.

Mortality Schedules

Mortality schedules were taken along with population schedules during the 1850, 1860, 1870, and 1880 censuses. They listed people who died between June 1 and May 31 in the previous year. Six states—Colorado, Florida, Nebraska, New Mexico, North Dakota, and South Dakota—had mortality schedules for the year 1885. A typical mortality schedule will list the dead person's name, age, sex, color (white, black, or mulatto); whether the person was married or widowed; birthplace; month of death; occupation; and cause of death.

Obituaries

Obituaries include some useful basic information, which is sometimes overlooked in the course of researching an ancestor.

Death Dates

An obituary provides a date of death—or at least a month and a year—and the town and/or county where the death occurred.

Last Known Place of Residence

An obituary will usually tell you the last place your ancestor resided. Obituaries can also tell you where the deceased's surviving family members were living at the time of his or her death. This can allow you to pick up the trail for surviving family members who left the area where the rest of their family were living.

Married Names for Daughters, Sisters, and Mothers

Obituaries can also provide important clues about female family members—for example, if a female family member married or remarried.

It's not unusual to discover that women in the family married more than once due to the premature death of a husband or divorce. This may explain why you might struggle to find women in additional records after a certain date.

Clarity on How to Spell an Ancestor's Name

Through an obituary, you can also confirm how your ancestor preferred to spell their name. This may seem insignificant, but it's important to honor your ancestors by using the form of their name they preferred and used.

Rich Details

You can also learn more about the person you are researching, such as their interests, hobbies, occupations, and achievements. This lifts their story above the usual dates of residence, birth, marriage, or death and begins to make them into three-dimensional people. In some cases, you may even discover a photograph of the person you are researching.

Obituaries can be accessed online from Ancestry, Chronicling America, FamilySearch, Legacy.com, Newspapers.com, and Obituaries.com. You may also find them in local and state archives and local newspaper archives as well as local historical and genealogical societies.

Researching coroner's records and finding obituaries may take some extra time and effort. But if you do find either of them, the reward may be useful genealogy clues that you can use to solve some family mysteries.

Obituaries and coroner's records just might lead you to your next discovery: the location of an ancestor's final resting place. In Step 44, we will look into the multitude of information you can find by visiting a cemetery where your ancestral family is buried.

STEP 44

Visit a Cemetery

You never know what you will discover when you visit a cemetery where a family is buried. Even if you're armed with information like birth and death dates, chances are you will make a new discovery or two.

You may stumble across the small graves of children who weren't otherwise documented in any records. Likewise, you may make a connection between people who bore the same surname who were buried close to one another, suggesting a kinship between them.

You may even find that a tombstone's bears a Mason's mark, leading you to visit the local lodge, which might hold records confirming that your ancestor—and several others—was indeed a member of the Freemasons. That lodge might also hold other records that provide more genealogical information about your ancestor.

Alternatively, an ancestor's tombstone might cite a religious affiliation or bear a religious symbol. This clue can help you determine the church where your ancestor worshipped, which might hold records for that ancestor and his or her family.

Lastly, a tombstone may bear a military service mark, which, again, would provide an additional avenue for you to research.

Items left on the grave, such as fresh flowers, might indicate descendants who live nearby. These living relations, if unknown to you, could provide invaluable information about your ancestors and their family.

Few things will give you a stronger feeling of connection to your ancestors than visiting their final resting place. It is a profoundly emotional and amazing experience. Just as amazing are the discoveries that you can make, like finding a previously undocumented child or an unknown first spouse.

OUR MOTHER
ANN MARIAH CHAMBERS
DIED

5 Tips for Visiting Cemeteries

1 Wear a pair of boots with long trousers and a long-sleeve shirt! Overgrown or abandoned rural cemeteries can be home to poisonous snakes, ticks, scorpions, and biting insects. Hats are a good idea, too.

2 Either take a long stick with you or find one outside the cemetery you visit. Beat the ground with it as you walk around. The noise will likely scare away snakes and other animals that could harm you.

3 Bring a bottle of water to keep yourself hydrated.

4 Check for ticks before you get into your car.

5 Before you visit, check with the county or organization that is responsible for the cemetery. Ask if it is permissible for you to bring a small, soft-bristled brush to remove debris from fallen tombstones to better enable you to read them. Remember, old and ancient tombstones are very, very delicate, so handle with care.

WOOL
Kerry

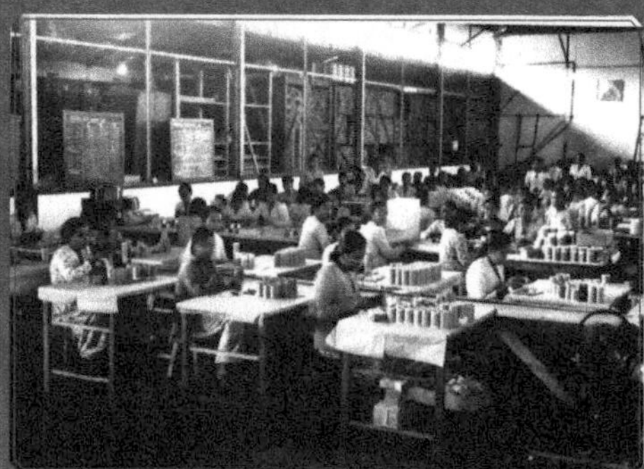

STEP 45

Investigate an Industry

Whether your family tree is filled with hard-working laborers, skilled craftsmen, talented seamstresses, passionate teachers, respected religious leaders, down-to-earth farmers, military servicemen, or fearless sailors, learning about your ancestors' occupations can take your genealogy to the next level. Knowing what it took to become successful in an industry will tell you something about the grit, fortitude, determination, and talents your ancestors possessed.

Why Research Occupations and Industries?

So why are occupations so important anyway? And what does learning about a profession have to do with genealogy? Identifying and knowing your ancestor's occupation can lead to some fantastic insights into their life. For example:

- Occupations can help you differentiate your ancestor from other people with the same name in public records. You might even learn about some special talents that they possessed.
- You may identify other records to search. Certain occupations have their own repositories of documents. For example, the railroad industry has a wealth of employee records available for access online and offline. Similarly, if your ancestor worked in an industry with union affiliations, his or her membership file may still exist.

A little research will help you understand what you ancestors' daily lives were like. Understanding what they did for a living is a good way to get a glimpse into their economic standing in the community.

There may be a link between an ancestor's occupation in America and their livelihood in the country of their birth, which could make for an interesting story. Keep this in mind as you familiarize yourself with how to write about your family's ethnic or immigrant story, the subject of Step 46.

Researching Occupations and Industries

1 Find their line of work

There are a variety of records that cite a person's occupation or trade:

- Tax lists
- Census records
- Obituaries
- City directories
- Military records
- Passenger lists
- Death and probate records
- Photographs (Did your ancestor pose for a work photo?)
- Old maps (which might identify a mill, school, factory, mine, etc., that an ancestor owned or was employed by)

2 Discover more about their trade/industry

Depending on the time period and the trade your ancestor was employed in, you may be able to learn details about what was involved in the type of work they did.

You will see terms in old records that apply to jobs that no longer exist. An Internet search may help you find out more about the industry your ancestor was engaged in. For example, you can search for phrases like "What is a cooper?" or "What was it like to run a rooming house?" or "What was it like to run a stagecoach business?"

You can also learn more details about historical occupations in history books and documentaries.

3 Look for resources and records

You may find historical books, documentaries, or even museum exhibits about the industry or the employer/business your ancestor owned or worked for, if it was a large business. Smaller businesses can be found in local or regional history books.

Try doing an Internet search using the names of family businesses or the type of business your ancestor was engaged in—such as tailor, hotel, sharecropping, or saloon—and the name of the town and state. You can include the word "history" to further narrow your search results.

STEP 46

Write Your Family's Ethnic/Immigrant Story

Writing about how an ancestor's ethnicity or immigration experience shaped their life in America can be powerful and moving.

Storytelling, however, is not without its challenges. Portraying the political, social, and economic factors that prompted an ancestor to leave the Old Country requires diligence and careful research. Also, bringing a bygone era to life in an authentic way is no easy matter.

The same is true when writing about how an ancestor's ethnicity shaped their life experience and the lives of their family.

> *The immigrant experience wasn't the same for the millions of people who came to America over the centuries. Nor was the experience of people from different ethnic backgrounds the same. Each story of immigration and ethnicity is unique.*

Following are six steps for you to consider when writing your family history.

6 Tips for Writing Your Family History

Before you can write a compelling story, you must gather some crucial information:

1 Research the country your immigrant ancestor left and/or the ethnic community to which your ancestor belonged. Write about the fundamental factors that shaped that community or place when your ancestor lived there.

- Geography: Describe the geography.
- Society: Describe the social customs and traditions.
- Politics: Examine the political landscape at the time of your ancestor's birth and during their formative years. Was your ancestor's family targeted because of their culture or ethnicity?
- Environment: Explore any famines or natural disasters that affected your family in the Old Country. Did a natural disaster affect your ancestor's family disproportionally compared to other families due to their ethnicity?

2 Research the motivational factors that prompted your immigrant ancestor's decision to leave their homeland, including religious, economic, ethnic, or cultural reasons.

3 Explore the other available destination options. For example, why did one ancestor go to America in the late 1800s when a sibling chose to immigrate to Argentina?

4 Investigate how life in America compared to life in the Old Country for your ancestors. Step 2: What's Your Starting Point? (page 5) and Step 3: Stay Organized (page 10) could help form the basis for this comparison. Was your ancestor able to continue in their same occupation? Did a change in geography play a role in their new life?

5 Look into how your ancestors traveled. What route did they take from their old home to their new one? What were the hardships—including cultural differences—they had to endure during their travel, and what obstacles did they have to overcome?

6 What kind of world awaited them when they arrived? What was the political situation in America when your ancestor arrived there? Social and cultural factors, historical tensions (e.g., Revolutionary War, Civil War, the Great Depression, etc.), persecution, and other historical events in America would all make excellent issues to explore.

Regardless of whether you plan to write a nonfiction or fiction book, an article, or a series of blog posts, you need to evaluate the facts you have extracted from your information sources and assemble them into a compelling narrative that conveys both the drama and individuality of your ancestor's immigration or ethnic, cultural experience.

Chances are your immigrant ancestors didn't arrive in America empty-handed. If they did bring precious mementos or a trinket from their home country and those artifacts still remain in your family, you have an heirloom—a treasured item that has been passed down through the generations of your family. You can also create new heirlooms honoring your family's ancestry, which is what we will explore more about in Step 47.

W PETERS
FID·DEF·IND·IMP
CROWN·1937
HALF CROWN

STEP 47

Make a Family Heirloom

4 Steps to Make a Family Heirloom

1 Quality

When it comes to furniture, jewelry, and artwork, quality is a crucial consideration. Can it stand the test of time? Is it durable?

2 Has a story

Does the object have a story, like the time great-grandpa's flask stopped a bullet in World War I? Or third great-grandma Sally's apple pie recipe? A story adds interest and a "wow" factor to heirlooms, making them truly unique.

3 Futureproof

Will the object be easy to pass down to future generations? How will you instill a sense of importance or pride in the object? How will the heirloom be stored or maintained?

4 Protection

Do you want the heirloom to pass from generation to generation? From mothers to daughters? From fathers to sons? Where will the object be stored and maintained? Establish the rules early on to avoid conflicts within the family and maintain the heirloom's safekeeping.

Heirlooms need not be priceless works of art, jewelry, silver settings, or furniture. Family recipes, photographs, letters, postcards, a bound copy of your family research logs, and more all make exceptional items to pass down through the generations within your family. Whatever form the heirloom takes, the emotional connection it has to your family will be what gives your heirloom its value.

> *Some heirlooms represent overcoming a struggle. Forced or compelled to leave their homeland, what things did your ancestors choose to bring with them for their new life in America? What object survives to represent a story of migration? Books, an ancestor's drinking flask, a pocket watch, military medals, or even a humble trunk can all be a testament to people who fled their home to start anew somewhere else.*

Sometimes, it is the story or stories that are attached to an heirloom that make the heirloom interesting and ensure that it will be passed down through the generations of a family. Your third great-grandmother's locket might be simple in its design and tarnished from age. However, the story of how she kept it safe on her journey from Poland will be priceless!

A family history book that includes information about your family can also make a great heirloom. You may have discovered a reference to just such a book. However, is it out of print? What should you do if you'd like to add this out-of-print book to your family's heirloom collection? We'll be exploring some answers to that question in Step 48.

STEP 48

Track Down Out-of-Print Items

You discovered a reference about an old local history book that has a chapter about your family. However, you've also found that the book has been out of print for decades. What do you do now? Don't give up or despair.

There are some simple tricks that can help you track down copies of out-of-print books.

While it may take some effort and plenty of patience to find out-of-print books and magazines, perseverance can really pay dividends. You may find the answers you are seeking to long-standing questions and, perhaps, find new information that leads you to new areas of research about your family.

- Google Books provides information about the author, publisher, ISBN, and more. You may also be able to access the material itself if it has been digitized.
- Archive.org and JSTOR offer free access to out-of-print books, magazines, etc.
- Write to the publisher, making sure to include the book title, author name, publication year, edition number (if applicable), and ISBN.
- Search the BookFinder, Wipf and Stock Publishers, and Ingram iPage websites for old titles.
- Search the WorldCat and Library of Congress websites for information on the title.

STEP 49

Bring Your Research Logs to Life

If you have been maintaining and updating your research logs, you will have the basis for writing about your family. You will have created an information repository you can easily access to write and share your family history. You will know the subject matter. Your timeline will contain the main story plot points. Additional contextual research, such as what your ancestor did for an occupation and how that occupation shaped their life, will add depth and flavor to the story. The images and digital copies of records you have collected will pack a visual punch.

After you've been researching your family for any significant length of time, few will know your family's story as you do. You will be adding to your family's legacy in a real and tangible way through your writing. Writing makes the history of your family more concrete and less likely to be forgotten.

Family history is history on a smaller scale. The story about how your seventh great-grandmother, Betsey Johnston, gave Captain John Smith's battalion two cows and a dozen chickens during the Revolutionary War may not seem like an interesting or monumental story to share. However, if she only owned three cows and two dozen chickens at the time, that's a story of sacrifice for the birth of the American dream. The tale of your second great-uncle Moses registering to vote in the first election after he was freed from slavery might also seem like an uninteresting story. However, when you realize he had dreamed of doing something as simple as voting for as long as he'd been enslaved, that makes the act of voter registration moving and meaningful.

As you have discovered throughout this book, family history goes beyond the names and dates you uncover through your research. It's history that makes us who we are. It's about people from our family's past with whom we can form a deep and profound connection. A family's history is about the people who lived and breathed—and possibly suffered and hopefully triumphed—in their lifetimes. It's about the roots and branches and leaves that make up your family tree. Those stories are about all of us.

Happy writing!

---

10 Steps to Write Your Family Story

1 Define the scope of your project

First, decide who to write about. Will it be an individual or a family? Will you go from the oldest-known ancestor to more recent family members? A group of ancestral families in a specific county or community? Your grandparents?

2 Choose a writing format

What form will your writing project take? You will need to match your personal interest in writing your family history with a potential audience.

- Narrative fiction
- Memoir
- History
- Biography
- Cookbook
- Scrapbook
- Newsletter

Or you may decide to write a mash-up type of book that combines multiple styles.

Your intended audience will also influence your decision. If it's limited to your immediate family, you may decide to write a fact-rich pamphlet. If your story has more of a universal appeal, a book or a website could be a good choice to consider.

3 Choose an engaging plot or theme

Think about your ancestors as characters in a story that just so happens to be about your family.

- Make it relatable for your audience.
- Did your ancestors overcome obstacles that could provide a good plotline, such as
    - Hitting the wagon trail?
    - A story of immigration?
    - A multigenerational story of going from poverty to business ownership?
    - Life in Alabama versus life in Michigan during the Great Migration?

4 Make a timeline

While you don't have to write your story in chronological order, timelines are important for keeping an ancestor's or family's major life events straight in your head.

Timelines can also prompt you to do some additional research on things such as how a war, a natural disaster, or religious turmoil in a foreign country influenced where your ancestor settled in the United States.

Additional reading on subjects like the typical foods of the time period, fashion, music, art, and culture can add additional context to the story of your ancestors' lives.

5 Do additional background research

Additional background research adds context to your ancestor's or family's story. It's the little details that will make your story truly engaging. Context will take a reader from being a bystander to being a participant or a witness.

What did that calico dress that your third great-grandmother made feel like? How much of her disposable income did it cost to buy the material? How did she find the time to make it with a household of eight children and farm work to do? It's tiny details like this that lift the level of interest in a story.

Add records and documents, if this is applicable.

6 Be specific

Adding relevant event or time period details can also raise the level of interest in a story. However, don't go off on a tangent. The background or contextual information you provide in your writing should add to the interest level or further a reader's understanding.

7 Find your voice

Write in your own voice. It's your passion that will bring your writing project to life and add authenticity to what you are writing. Also, give yourself a break: It can take years for a writer to find his or her writing "voice." The process of discovering your writing style will probably feel awkward at first. The more you consistently work on your writing, the more the initial awkwardness will start to fade away.

8 Include sensory triggers for your readers

Add descriptions that touch on the five senses to lift an event from the mundane to the memorable. Think about how you would have felt in or responded to a specific situation you are writing about. Try visiting the place where your ancestor lived. Walk around and really engage your five senses as you do so, noting everything down in a notebook that you can refer back to when you begin to write.

9 Include references and citations

Source citations are an essential part of writing. They provide credibility to your research and enable readers to verify your findings.

10 Set realistic deadlines

If writing one chapter a week is all you can realistically do, then don't push yourself to write two.

Schedule "writing time" when you can consistently sit down and write. Tell your family and friends that you'd like to avoid interruption during this time. Once you start writing, you will be able to determine what a realistic writing schedule will look like for you.

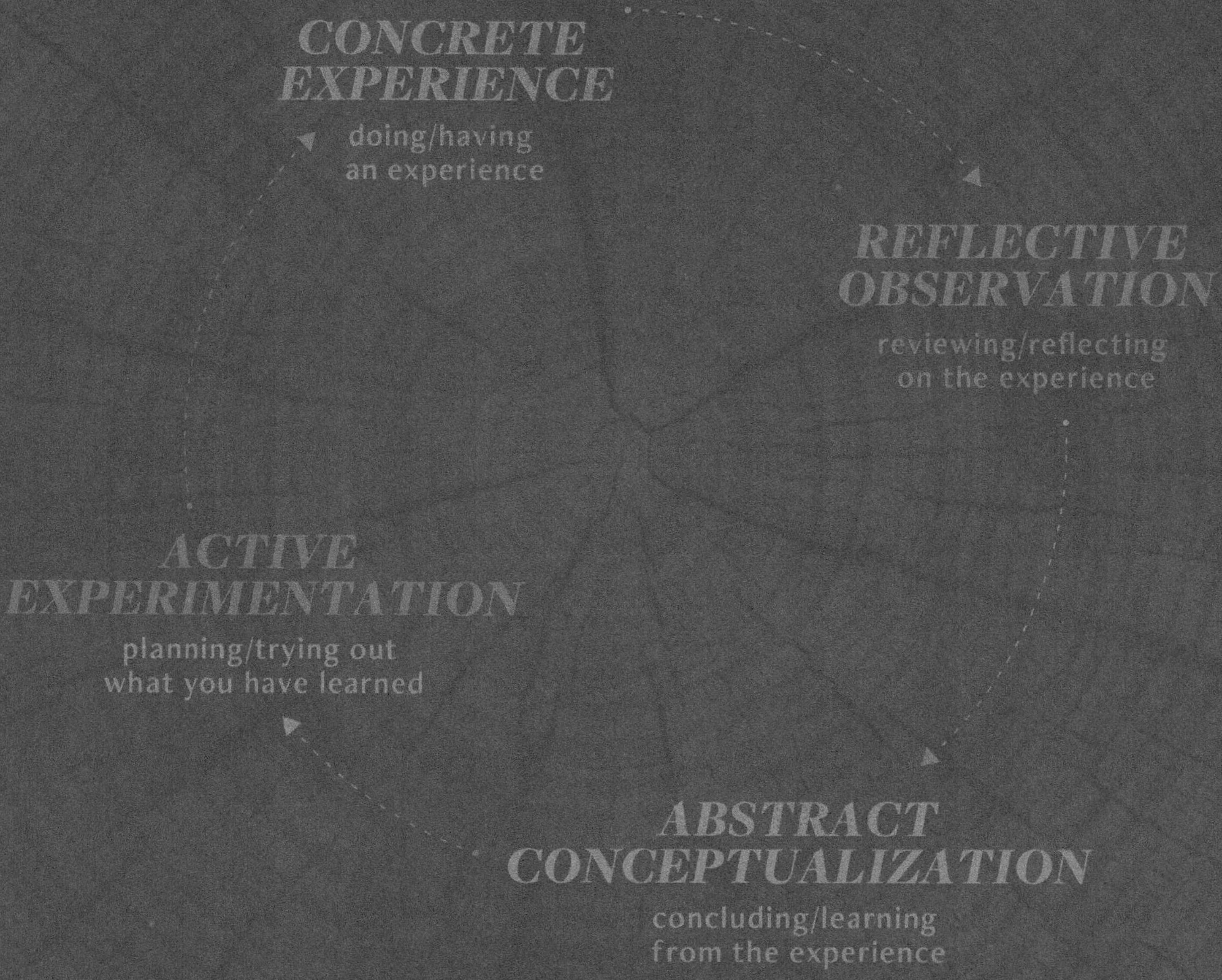
CONCRETE EXPERIENCE
doing/having an experience
REFLECTIVE OBSERVATION
reviewing/reflecting on the experience
ABSTRACT CONCEPTUALIZATION
concluding/learning from the experience
ACTIVE EXPERIMENTATION
planning/trying out what you have learned

STEP 50

Reflect

REFLECT

Take some time to reflect upon the new skills and information we have covered.

Check in with yourself by answering the following questions:

- How well do you understand exploring your heritage and ethnicity?
- Are you able to identify sources of information that tell the story of how your ancestors moved from one place to another? How familiar are you with the potential hardships your ancestors faced?
- How confident are you in finding documents and information that tell your ancestors' backstories (e.g., their occupation or career)?
- How confident are you that you can turn your research into a written history of your family?

Give yourself permission to acknowledge if you are still unclear about a topic that we have explored together. Reread previous steps if you need to. Remember, genealogy is an endurance activity. It isn't a sprint.

Make sure you really understand and can apply the concepts we have explored up to this point.

All the best in your genealogy adventures!

APPENDIX A

FINDING A LOST CONNECTION TO THE WEEPING TIME SLAVE SALE

(1859, SAVANNAH, GEORGIA)

This case study represents a real-world example of creating a research outline with specific goals and steps. While this case study is specific to researching enslaved African American ancestors, the method is also applicable for non–African American researchers.

Research Questions

The research questions are: Why do DNA test results for interrelated family groups in the Old Ninety-Six District of South Carolina show a trace amount of Gullah DNA? and Who are the unknown ancestors who connect descendants in the Old Ninety-Six District of South? The Gullah community lives along the coastal South Carolina and Georgia region—hundreds of miles from the Old Ninety-Six District. Initial research and DNA test results show a connection to the enslaved people held by Major Pierce Butler and his grandson, Pierce Mease Butler.

Research Goals and Steps

Identify the Research Focus

1 **Identify** the 440 enslaved people (EPs) sold by Pierce Mease Butler during the three-day 1859 sale in Savannah referred to as the Weeping Time sale.

2 **Identify** the enslaved people not put up for sale by Pierce Mease Butler.

Conduct Background Reading and Focused Research

1 **Read.** The research team will need to do a substantial amount of reading about Pierce Mease Butler, the Weeping Time sale, and the history of the Butler plantations in South Carolina and Georgia. This is one way to acquire the names of the individuals and families enslaved by the Butler family.

2 **Research** the history of enslaving within the earlier generations of the Butler family and any allied families, with a specific focus on Pierce Mease Butler's maternal grandfather, Major Pierce Butler. Maj. Butler is a key person in this history, which explains the focus on him in particular. This stage includes:

- Create a family tree covering Pearse Mease Butler's lineage, including listing and researching all the families and individuals enslaved by them.
- Locate and transcribe family wills, estate inventories, lawsuits, slave mortgages, slave insurance policies, deeds of purchase and sale for the enslaved, farm books/day books, journals, letters, etc. This allows researchers to trace which family members received which enslaved people over five to six generations.
- Locate and transcribe Maj. Butler's slave register entries covering the 1775 to 1815 time period. This is important for researching the people held by the family.
- Find and transcribe the list of enslaved people held by Maj. Butler who went away with the British during the Revolutionary War.
- Find and transcribe the 1815 list of enslaved people held by Maj. Butler who went away with the British.
- Find and transcribe Maj. Butler's birth and death lists for his enslaved people (1800–1834).
- Find and digitize purchases and sales of Maj. Butler's enslaved people.
- Find and digitize the weekly reports sent from the overseers in South Carolina and Georgia to Maj. Butler in Philadelphia. These reports will contain information about the enslaved.
- Map the EPs held by Maj. Pierce Butler to the EPs his wife, Mary Middleton, and their children inherited from Mary Middleton Butler's South Carolina grandmother, Mary Branford Bull.
- Map the EPs held by Maj. Pierce Butler back to the EPs who were inherited by Mary Bull Middleton's other children but were in the possession of Maj. Pierce Butler.
- Map the EPs held by Maj. Butler to the Africans who were imported into Charleston by Maj. Butler and his relations via marriage, the Bull and Middleton families.

Each of the preceding steps listed leads to a goal that can answer the two research questions stated at the beginning of the research plan.

APPENDIX B

CITATION FORMATS BY INFORMATION SOURCE TYPE

Articles (Journal or Periodical)

Citations for periodicals should include the month/year or season rather than issue number, where possible.

Willis H. White, "Using Uncommon Sources to Illuminate Family History: A Long Island Tuthill Example." *National Genealogical Society Quarterly* 91 (March 2003), 15–18.

Bible Records

Citations for information found in a family Bible should always include the information on publication and its provenance (names and dates for people who have owned the Bible).

Family data, Dempsey Owens Family Bible, The Holy Bible (American Bible Society, New York 1853); original owned in 2001 by William L. Owens [put mailing address here]. The Dempsey Owens Family Bible passed from Dempsey to his son James Turner Owens, to his son Dempsey Raymond Owens, to his son William L. Owens.

Birth and Death Certificates

When citing a birth or death record, record the type of record and name(s) of the individual(s), the file or certificate number (or book and page), and the name and location of the office in which it is filed or the repository in which the copy was found (e.g., archives).

Henrietta Crisp, birth certificate [long form] no. 124-83-001153 (1983), North Carolina Division of Health Services—Vital Records Branch, Raleigh.

From an Online Index

Ohio Death Certificate Index 1913–1937, The Ohio Historical Society, online http://www.ohiohistory.org/dindex/search.cfm, Death certificate entry for Eveline Powell downloaded 12 March 2001.

From an FHL Microfilm

Yvonne Lemarie entry, Crespières naissances, mariages, déecs 1893–1899, microfilm no. 2067622 Item 6, frame 58, Family History Library [FHL], Salt Lake City, Utah.

Books

Published sources, including books, should list author (or compiler or editor) first followed by the title, publisher, publication place and date, and page numbers. List multiple authors in the same order as shown on the title page, unless there are more than three authors—in which case, include only the first author followed by "et al." Citations for one volume of a multivolume work should include the number of the volume used.

Margaret M. Hoffman, compiler, *The Granville District of North Carolina*, 1748–1763, 5 volumes (Weldon, North Carolina: Roanoke News Company, 1986), 1:25, no. 238*.

*The number in this example indicates a specific numbered entry on the page.

Census Records

While it is tempting to abbreviate many items in a census citation, especially state name and county designations, it is best to spell out all words in the first citation to a particular census. Abbreviations which seem standard to you (e.g., *Co.* for county) may not be recognized by all researchers.

1920 U.S. census, population schedule, Brookline, Norfolk County, Massachusetts, Enumeration District [ED] 174, sheet 8, dwelling 110, family 172, Frederick A. Kerry household; National Archives microfilm publication T625, roll 721; digital image, Ancestry.com, http://www.ancestry.com (Accessed 28 July 2004).

Family Group Sheets

When you use information which has been received from others, you should always document the data as you receive it and not use the original sources cited by the other researcher. You haven't personally checked these sources, therefore they should not be listed as your source.

Jane Doe, "William M. Crisp–Lucy Cherry family group sheet," supplied 2 February 2001 by Doe [put mailing address here].

Interviews

Be sure to document who you interviewed and when as well as who is in possession of any interview records, such as transcripts, tape recordings, etc.

Interview with Charles Bishop Koth [interviewee's address here], by Kimberly Thomas Powell, 7 August 1999. Transcript held in 2001 by Powell [put mailing address here]. [You can include an annotation or personal comment here.]

Letters

It is much more accurate to quote a specific letter as a source rather than just citing the individual who wrote the letter as your source.

Letter from Patrick Owens [put mailing address here] to Kimberly Thomas Powell, 9 January 1998; held in 2001 by Powell [put mailing address here]. [You can include an annotation or personal comment here.]

Marriage Licenses or Certificates

Marriage records follow the same general format as birth and death records.

Marriage license and certificate for Dempsey Owens and Lydia Ann Everett, Edgecombe County Marriage Book 2:36, County Clerk's Office, Tarboro, North Carolina.

George Frederick Powell and Rosina Jane Powell, Bristol Marriage Register 1:157, Bristol Register Office, Bristol, Gloucestershire, England.

Newspaper Clippings

Be sure to include the name of the newspaper, the place and date of publication, and the page and column number.

Henry Charles Koth–Mary Elizabeth Ihly marriage announcement, *Southern Baptist* newspaper, Charleston, South Carolina, 16 June 1860, page 8, column 1.

Websites

This general citation format applies to information received from Internet databases as well as online transcriptions and indexes. For example, if you find a cemetery transcription on the Internet, you would enter it as a website source. You would not include the cemetery as your source unless you had visited it personally.

Wuerttemberg Emigration Index, Ancestry.com, online https://www.ancestry.com/search/collections/3141/, Koth data downloaded 12 January 2000.

Pictures and Home Movies

To create a citation for an image, include the following information:

- The name of the creator of the image or home movie
- The title of the digital image or home movie (alternatively, you can include a description of the image instead)
- The title of the website, book, or collection or the name of the person who has provided the image or movie to you
- The names of any other contributors responsible for the image or movie (if applicable)
- Version of the image or movie (if applicable)
- The publisher of the image or movie
- The date the image or movie was created or published
- The location of the image or movie (i.e., the URL for the image or physical location where it can be found. If in private hands, you can exclude the street address; however, note the town and state.)

Creator's Last name, First name. "Title of the digital image." *Title of the website*, First name Last name of any contributors, Version (if applicable), Number (if applicable), Publisher, Publication date, URL.

GLOSSARY

ABSTRACT: An abbreviated transcription of a document that includes the date of the record and every name it contains; it may also provide relationships or descriptions (witness, executor, bondsman, son, widow) of the people who are mentioned.

ALIQUOT PARTS: A description for an exact subdivision of a section of land in the rectangular survey system. Aliquot parts use directions and fractions to indicate the land's location—for example, "S ½ NW ¼" represents the southern half of the northwest quarter of a township.

ANCESTORS: The relatives you descend from directly, including your parents, grandparents, great-grandparents, and so on. Your number of ancestors doubles each generation you move backward. For example, you have four grandparents, eight great-grandparents, and 16 great-great-grandparents.

AUTOSOMAL DNA: Genetic material inherited equally from both parents. It's less useful genealogically than Y-DNA and mtDNA because it mutates more often.

BANNS (OR MARRIAGE BANNS): Church-generated documents publicly stating couples' intent to marry. The custom dates back to colonial America. Banns were posted or read on three consecutive Sundays.

BLOCK NUMBER: A one-, two-, or three-digit number that describes a block (or piece) of land within a township.

BOND: A written, signed, and witnessed agreement requiring someone to pay a specified amount of money by a given date.

BOUNTY LAND: Land granted by the colonial and federal governments as a reward for military service. Bounty-land warrants—documents granting the right to the land—were assigned to soldiers, their heirs, and other individuals.

BUREAU OF LAND MANAGEMENT GENERAL LAND OFFICE (GLO): The U.S. government office historically responsible for the disposal of public land. Usually, several branch land offices existed for each state.

CEMETERY RECORDS: Records of the names and death dates of those buried in a cemetery as well as maps of grave sites, usually kept by cemetery caretakers. More-detailed records, including the names of the deceased's relatives, may also be included.

CENSUS: An official count of the population in a particular area. The census generally collects other details as well, such as names, ages, citizenship status, and ethnic background. The U.S. government began collecting census data in 1790 and has done so every 10 years since then.

Selected states have also conducted their own censuses over the years.

CERTIFIED COPY: A copy made and attested to by officers who are responsible for keeping the original record or document and who are authorized to give copies.

CHROMOSOME: A threadlike strand of DNA that carries genes and transmits hereditary information.

CLUSTER GENEALOGY: The study of ancestors as part of a group, or "cluster," of relatives, friends, neighbors, and associates. The cluster approach can help you find or confirm details you might miss by looking only at an individual ancestor.

COLLATERAL RELATIVE: Any kin who aren't in your direct line, such as siblings, aunts, uncles, and cousins.

CREDIT PATENT: A document transferring land to be paid for in installments over a four-year period. A delinquent payment or nonpayment of the full balance resulted in forfeiture. In 1820, Congress required full payment for land at the time of purchase.

DECLARATION OF INTENTION: An alien's sworn statement that he or she wants to become a citizen of the United States; also called "first papers." Declarations were filed in federal court and list personal details such as name, age, occupation, birthplace, and last foreign residence.

DEED: A document transferring ownership and title of property. Unlike a patent, a deed records the sale of property from one private individual to another.

DESCENDANT REPORT: Similar to an Outline Descendant Chart, this report also includes dates and places of birth, death, and burial and displays detailed information on a person's descendants in a compact format.

DESCENDANTS: An ancestor's offspring: children, grandchildren, and every new generation in the direct line.

DNA: The molecule that contains each cell's genetic code, organized into 23 pairs of chromosomes. Genetic genealogy tests analyze your Y-DNA, mtDNA, or autosomal DNA.

DOCUMENTATION: The process of citing your sources of family history information. Thorough documentation helps you keep track of the details and sources you've researched and allows other researchers to verify your findings.

ENUMERATION DISTRICTS: Divisions of each county and some large cities used to make census-taking more efficient and accurate. For large cities, the boundaries of enumeration districts often match those of wards or precincts.

FAMILY GROUP RECORD (OR SHEET): Succinctly summarizes information on a couple and their children, including names; dates and places of birth, baptism, marriage, death and burial; and source citations.

FREEDMAN: A man or woman who was freed from slavery; an emancipated person.

GENE: A hereditary unit consisting of a sequence of DNA that occupies a specific location on a chromosome.

GENEALOGY: The study of your family's history and the process of tracing your ancestors back through time.

HAPLOGROUP: An identification of the genetic group your ancient ancestors belonged to, going back 10,000 to 60,000-plus years

HOMESTEAD: A home on land obtained from the U.S. government. Homesteaders were required to live on the land and make improvements, such as adding buildings and clearing fields.

HOMESTEAD ACT OF 1862: A law allowing people to settle up to 160 acres of public land if they lived on it for five years and grew crops or made improvements. The land was free, aside from a filing fee.

INDEX: An alphabetical list of names taken from a particular set of records. For example, a census index lists the names of people named in a particular set of census records, such as the 1870 or 1900 census. Indexes come in book form and on CD, microfilm, and microfiche.

INTERNATIONAL GENEALOGICAL INDEX (IGI): One of the resources of the Family History Library of the Church of Jesus Christ of Latter-Day Saints. The Index consists of approximately 250 million names that were either submitted to the church or extracted from records that the church has microfilmed over the years.

INTESTATE: Having died without leaving a will.

LAND CLAIM: A settler's application to receive public land.

LAND-ENTRY CASE FILE: A file created when a person claimed land under an act of Congress, such as the Homestead Act of 1862, which includes information such as marriage or immigration documents; receipts; and affidavits of occupation, immigration, marriage, and homestead application.

LAND GRANT: Public land given to an individual by the government, usually as a reward for military service.

LAND PATENT: A document transferring land ownership from the federal government to an individual.

LEGACY: Property or money bequeathed to someone in a will.

LEGAL LAND DESCRIPTION: In a land patent, an exact identification of the land being transferred using survey terms

LIEN: A claim placed on property by a person who is owed money.

LOCAL HISTORY: Typically, a book about a town or county.

MANUSCRIPTS: Handwritten documents and records—such as diaries, letters, or family Bible entries—that can contain items relating to family, business, or organization papers. These items are listed by the National Union Catalog of Manuscript Collections (NUCMC).

MEDICAL RECORDS: Records and files associated with a patient's medical treatment (including at mental asylums), which may not be accessible to the public due to privacy protections.

MERIDIAN: An imaginary north-south line. A principal meridian is the starting point for a rectangular land survey.

METES AND BOUNDS: A land survey method employing compass directions, natural landmarks, and distances between points.

MILITARY RECORDS: Documents relating to military service. These records fall into two categories—compiled service records and veterans' benefits—and can include volunteer records, pension and bounty-land warrant applications, draft registration cards, and military discharge papers. These have been kept by the U.S. federal government since the American Revolution.

MIRACODE SYSTEM: A computer-generated indexing system used to organize the 1910 census results. Index cards are computer generated, organized first by Soundex code, then alphabetically by county, and then alphabetically by given name.

MITOCHONDRIAL DNA: Genetic material both males and females inherit from their mothers.

MORTALITY SCHEDULE: A section of the federal census listing information about persons who died during the census year.

NATIONAL ARCHIVES AND RECORDS ADMINISTRATION (NARA): The U.S. archive of all federal records, including census records, military service rolls, pension applications, passenger lists, and bounty-land warrants. Located in Washington, DC, the archive also has 13 regional facilities across the nation.

NATURALIZATION RECORDS: Documents of the process by which an immigrant became a citizen of the United States, which provide the individual's birthplace and date, arrival date, place of residence at the time of naturalization, and personal description. These records can also include the name of the ship on which the person arrived (if applicable) and the immigrant's occupation.

ORAL HISTORY: A collection of family stories told by a member of the family or by a close family friend.

PASSENGER LIST: A list of the names and information about passengers who arrived in the United States on ships submitted to customs collectors at every port by the ship's master.

PEDIGREE: A list of a person's ancestors.

PENSION (MILITARY): A benefit paid regularly to a veteran or his widow for military service or a military service–related disability.

PLAT: A drawing that shows the boundaries and features of a piece of property. In genealogy, platting refers to creating such a drawing from a metes-and-bounds or legal land description as a surveyor would have done.

PRIMARY SOURCE: A record or other source created at the time of a particular event. A primary source is always the original record.

PROBATE RECORDS: Records of the disposition of a deceased person's property, which may include a last will and testament and estate inventories.

PUBLIC LAND: Land originally owned by the federal government and sold to individuals.

QUAKER: A member of the religious group called the Society of Friends.

QUARTER SECTION: In the rectangular survey system, one-fourth of a section of land, equal to 160 acres.

RANGE: A row or column of townships lying east or west of the principal meridian, numbered successively to the east and to the west from the principal meridian.

REAL PROPERTY: Land and anything attached to it, such as houses, buildings, barns, growing timber, and growing crops.

RECTANGULAR SURVEY SYSTEM: The land survey method used most frequently by the General Land Office. This method employs base lines, one east-west and one north-south, that cross at a known geographic position. Two large rectangles, called townships—each generally 36 miles square—are described in relation to the base lines.

SECONDARY SOURCE: A record created after an event occurred, such as a biography, local history, index, oral history interview, or computer database.

SECTION: A division of land within a township that measures one square mile (640 acres)—about $\frac{1}{36}$ of a township. Sections were further subdivided into half sections, quarter sections, and sixteenth sections or into lots.

SOCIAL SECURITY DEATH INDEX: An index of Social Security death records, usually names of deceased Social Security recipients whose relatives applied for Social Security Death Benefits.

SOUNDEX: A system of coding surnames based on how they sound, which was used to index the 1880 and later censuses. Soundex cards are arranged first by Soundex code, then alphabetically by given name, and then (if necessary) alphabetically by place of birth.

STATE LAND: Land originally owned by a state or other entity rather than the federal government

TOWNSHIP: In a government survey, a square tract measuring six miles on each side (total 36 square miles); also a name given to the civil and political subdivisions of a county.

TRACT: A parcel of land that isn't fully contained within a single section. Tracts within a township are numbered beginning with 37 to avoid confusion with section numbers.

UNION LIST OR CATALOG: A bibliography or catalog of materials held by multiple libraries or repositories, such as the National Union Catalog of Manuscript Collections, a Library of Congress-generated finding aid for personal papers in institutions nationwide.

VISITATION NUMBER: The house number of the indexed individual found on a 1910 Miracode index card.

VITAL RECORDS: The most basic information available about a person. These statistics include birth (abbreviated *b*), marriage date and place (abbreviated *m*), divorce date and place (abbreviated *div*, if applicable), and death date and burial place (abbreviated *d* and *bur*).

VOLUME NUMBER: The number of the census volume in which the indexed name appears on a Soundex or Miracode index card.

VOTER REGISTRATION: A list of registered voters for each state. Sometimes these are the first public records of former slaves.

WILL: A document in which a person outlines what should be done with his or her estate after death.

WITNESS: A person who sees an event and signs a document attesting to its content being accurate.

X: What the signer of a document would often write if he or she couldn't write their name. A witness would typically label this "his mark."

Y CHROMOSOME: Genetic material passed down from father to son.

RESOURCES

Websites

THE AFRICAN AMERICAN NEWSPAPERS COLLECTION, BY ACCESSIBLE ARCHIVES: https://www.accessible-archives.com/collections/african-american-newspapers

AFRIGENEAS: http://www.afrigeneas.com

ANCESTRY.COM: https://www.ancestry.com

ARCHIVES.GOV: https://www.archives.gov

BOOKFINDER: https://www.bookfinder.com

THE BUREAU OF REFUGEES, FREEDMEN, AND ABANDONED LANDS (THE FREEDMEN'S BUREAU): https://www.familysearch.org/wiki/en/African_American_Freedmen%27s_Bureau_Records

CHRONICLING AMERICA: https://chroniclingamerica.loc.gov

CYNDI'S LIST: https://www.cyndislist.com

FAMILYPEDIA: https://familypedia.wikia.org

FAMILYSEARCH: https://www.familysearch.org

FAMILY TREE MAGAZINE: https://www.familytreemagazine.com

FIND A GRAVE: https://www.findagrave.com

FOLD3: https://www.fold3.com

GENEALOGYBANK: https://blog.genealogybank.com

GENEALOGYLINKS: http://www.genealogylinks.net

GOOGLE BOOKS: https://books.google.com

HISTORYLINES: https://www.historylines.com

INGRAM IPAGE: https://ipage.ingramcontent.com

INTERNATIONAL SOCIETY OF GENETIC GENEALOGY: https://www.isogg.org

INTERNET ARCHIVE: https://www.archive.org

JEWISHGEN: https://www.jewishgen.org

JSTOR: https://www.jstor.org

LIBRARY OF CONGRESS: https://www.loc.gov

LIBRARY OF VIRGINIA: http://www.lva.virginia.gov

LOWCOUNTRY AFRICANA: https://www.lowcountryafricana.com

MYHERITAGE: https://www.myheritage.com

MYTREES.COM: https://www.mytrees.com

AMERICAN ANCESTORS, BY THE NEW ENGLAND HISTORIC GENEALOGICAL SOCIETY: https://www.americanancestors.org

NEWSPAPERS.COM: https://www.newspapers.com

NOVA ONLINE TELEVISION, MYSTERY OF THE FIRST AMERICANS (BROADCAST TRANSCRIPT, AIRED FEB. 15, 2000), PBS

PINTEREST: https://www.pinterest.com

PREZI: https://www.prezi.com/

PROQUEST: https://www.proquest.com

PULLMAN EMPLOYEE RECORDS: https://www.newberry.org/pullman-employee-records

READEX: https://www.readex.com

ROBERTA ESTES' DNAEXPLAINED: https://www.dna-explained.com

ROOTSTECH: https://www.rootstech.org

ROOTSWEB: https://www.rootsweb.com

THOUGHTCO: https://www.thoughtco.com

TIKI-TOKI: https://www.tiki-toki.com

TIMETOAST: https://www.timetoast.com

UNKNOWN NO LONGER: https://www.virginiahistory.org/collections/unknown-no-longer-database-virginia-slave-names

UNITED STATES NATIONAL ARCHIVES: https://www.archives.gov

VITALREC: https://www.vitalrec.com

WIKITREE: https://www.wikitree.com

WIPF AND STOCK PUBLISHERS: http://www.wipf.com/

WORLDCAT: https://www.worldcat.org

Timeline Creation Services

HISTORYLINES: https://www.historylines.com

PINTEREST: https://www.pinterest.com. You can see an example I created using Pinterest, "John Fairman Preston: A Missionary's Life in Pins," via https://www.pinterest.com/genealogyadvent/john-fairman-preston-a-missionarys-life-in-pins

PREZI: https://www.prezi.com/

TIMETOAST: https://www.timetoast.com

TIKI-TOKI: https://www.tiki-toki.com

REFERENCES

Online Articles

Beidler, James M. "Genealogy Workbook: Tax Records." 2015. *Family Tree Magazine*. April 6, 2015. Accessed November 12, 2019. https://www.familytreemagazine.com/premium/genealogy-workbook-tax-records.

"Defining Critical Thinking." The Foundation for Critical Thinking. Accessed September 17, 2013. https://www.criticalthinking.org/pages/defining-critical-thinking/766.

DeGrazia, Laura M. "Skillbuilding: Planning Effective Research." 2015. Board for Certification of Genealogists. September 2015. https://bcgcertification.org/skillbuilding-planning-effective-research.

Estes, Roberta. "Concepts—Calculating Ethnicity Percentages." 2017. DNAeXplained—Genetic Genealogy. January 11, 2017. Accessed November 12, 2019. https://dna-explained.com/2017/01/11/concepts-calculating-ethnicity-percentages.

Evans, Stefani. "Skillbuilding: Data Analysis." 2012. Board For Certification Of Genealogists. May 2012. https://bcgcertification.org/skillbuilding-data-analysis.

Jackson, Kate. "100 Questions Every Family Historian Should Ask Their Relatives + A Free Printable List!" 2019. *Family History Daily*. September 13, 2019. https://familyhistorydaily.com/free-genealogy-resources/family-history-interview-questions.

Jones, Thomas W. "Skillbuilding: The Genealogical Proof Standard: How Simple Can It Be?" 2010. Board for Certification of Genealogists. September 2010. https://bcgcertification.org/skillbuilding-the-genealogical-proof-standard-how-simple-can-it-be.

"Land Records." 2019. National Archives. September 4, 2019. Accessed November 12, 2019. https://www.archives.gov/research/land.

"Lesson Plan—Culture, Race & Ethnicity." *Australian Government Department of Home Affairs*. https://www.harmony.gov.au/get-involved/schools/lesson-plans/lesson-plan-culture-race-ethnicity.

Little, Barbara V. "Skillbuilding: It's Not That Hard to Write Proof Arguments." 2009. Board for Certification of Genealogists. September 2009. https://bcgcertification.org/skillbuilding-its-not-that-hard-to-write-proof-arguments.

Mercedes. "What Do the Percentages on My Ethnicity Estimate Really Mean?" 2018. Who Are You Made Of? December 7, 2018. Accessed November 12, 2019. https://whoareyoumadeof.com/blog/2018/12/07/what-do-the-percentages-on-my-ethnicity-estimate-really-mean.

Miller, Gail J. "Skillbuilding: Finding the Truth in the Undocumented Story." 2017. Board for Certification of Genealogists. September 2017. https://bcgcertification.org/skillbuilding-truth-in-undocumented-story.

Mills, Elizabeth S. "Skillbuilding: Producing Quality Research Notes." 1997. Board for Certification of Genealogists. January 1997. https://bcgcertification.org/skillbuilding-producing-quality-research-notes.

Mills, Elizabeth S. "Skillbuilding: Transcribing Source Materials." 1996. Board for Certification of Genealogists. January 1996. https://bcgcertification.org/skillbuilding-transcribing-source-materials.

"Naturalization Records." 2016. National Archives. August 15, 2016. Accessed November 12, 2019. https://www.archives.gov/research/immigration/naturalization.

Powell, Kimberly. "How to Cite Genealogy Sources." 2019. ThoughtCo. Last modified March 31, 2019. Accessed November 12, 2019. https://www.thoughtco.com/how-to-cite-genealogy-sources-1421785.

Powell, Kimberly. "How US Public Land Is Surveyed and Distributed." 2019. ThoughtCo. Last modified March 08, 2019. Accessed November 12, 2019. https://www.thoughtco.com/section-township-and-range-land-records-1420632.

"Research Logs." 2018. FamilySearch Wiki. 2018. https://www.familysearch.org/wiki/en/Research_Logs.

Sheffey, Brian. "Critical Thinking: An Important Skill in Genealogy Research." 2017. Genealogy Adventures. July 24, 2017. https://genealogyadventures.net/2017/07/24/critical-thinking-an-important-skill-in-genealogy-research.

Sheffey, Brian. "Martha Ann Fowler Hill: Smashing Genealogy Walls with the Correct Maiden Name." 2015. Genealogy Adventures. April 8, 2015. https://genealogyadventures.net/2015/04/07/martha-fowler-hill-smashing-genealogy-walls-with-the-correct-maiden-name.

Sheffey, Brian. "My 18th Century Virginia Ball Family Genealogy Challenge." 2016. Genealogy Adventures. April 9, 2016. https://genealogyadventures.net/2016/04/09/my-18th-century-virginia-ball-family-genealogy-challenge.

Sheffey, Brian. "Recording Names: Maiden Names." 2011. Genealogy Adventures. October 24, 2011. https://genealogyadventures.net/2011/10/24/recording-names-maiden-names.

Sheffey, Brian. "William Holloway, Martha Branson and Phebe Crispin: A Genealogical Game of Hide and Seek." 2017. Genealogy Adventures. October 13, 2017. https://genealogyadventures.net/2017/10/13/william-holloway-martha-branson-phebe-crispin-a-genealogical-game-of-hide-and-seek.

"Vital Records—Birth Certificates, Death Records, Marriage Licenses and More." *Vitalrec*. Accessed November 12, 2019. http://vitalrec.com/index.html.

Books and Print Articles

Anderson, Margo J. *The American Census: A Social History*. New Haven, CT: Yale University Press, 2015.

Black, Henry C. *Black's Law Dictionary*. St. Paul, MN: West Publishing Company, 1990.

Carmack, Sharon D. *A Genealogist's Guide to Discovering Your Female Ancestors: Special Strategies for Uncovering Hard-to-Find Information about Your Female Lineage*. Cincinnati, OH: North Light Books, 1998.

Eicholz, Alice. *Red Book: American State, County, and Town Sources*. Salt Lake City, UT: Ancestry, 1992.

Foeman, Anita, Bessie Lee Lawton, and Randall Rieger. "Questioning Race: Ancestry DNA and Dialog on Race." *Communication Monographs* 82, no. 2 (2015): 271–90.

Hone, E. Wade. *Land & Property Research in the United States*. Provo, UT: Ancestry, 2008.

Kettner, James H. *The Development of American Citizenship, 1608–1870*. Chapel Hill, NC: University of North Carolina Press, 2014.

Gauthier, Jason G., and United States Census Bureau. *Measuring America: The Decennial Censuses from 1790 to 2000*. Washington, DC: U.S. Department of Commerce, U.S. Census Bureau, 2002.

LeMay, Michael C., and Elliot Robert Barkan. *U.S. Immigration and Naturalization Laws and Issues: A Documentary History*. Westport, CT: Greenwood Press, 1999.

Newman, John J. *American Naturalization Processes and Procedures, 1790–1985*. Indianapolis, IN: Indiana Historical Society, 1985.

Nordgren, A., and E. T. Juengst. "Can Genomics Tell Me Who I Am? Essentialistic Rhetoric in Direct-to-Consumer DNA Testing." *New Genetics and Society* 28, no. 2 (2009): 157–72.

Prechtel-Kluskens, Claire. "The Location of Naturalization Records." *The Record* 3, no. 2 (November 1996): 21–22.

Relethford, John. *Fundamentals of Biological Anthropology*. Mountain View, CA: McGraw-Hill, 1997.

Rose, Christine. *Courthouse Research for Family Historians: Your Guide to Genealogical Treasures*. San Jose, CA: CR Publications, 2004.

Rose, Christine. *Genealogical Proof Standard: Building a Solid Case, Revised, Enlarged Edition*. San Jose, CA: CR Publications, 2005.

Schaefer, Christina K. *Guide to Naturalization Records of the United States*. Baltimore, MD: Genealogical Publishing Company, 1997.

Staples, Brent. "The Shifting Meanings of 'Black' and 'White.'" *The New York Times*, November 15, 1998.

Thorndale, William, and William Dollarhide. *Map Guide to the U.S. Federal Censuses, 1790–1920*. Baltimore, MD: Genealogical Publishing Company, 1987.

Tutton, R. "'They Want to Know Where They Came From': Population Genetics, Identity, and Family Genealogy." *New Genetics and Society* 23, no. 1 (2004): 105–20.

U.S. Congress Joint Committee on Internal Revenue Taxation. *Legislative History of United States Tax Conventions*. Washington, DC: U.S. Government Printing Office, 1962.

U.S. General Services Administration. *Code of Federal Regulations: Record 2: 2007*. Washington, DC: National Archives and Records Service, Office of the Federal Register, 2008.

U.S. Internal Revenue Service. *Income Taxes 1862–1962: A History of the Internal Revenue Service*. Washington, DC: U.S. Government Printing Office, 1963.

U.S. National Center for Health Statistics. *Where to Write for Vital Records: Births, Deaths, Marriages, and Divorces*. Washington, DC: U.S. Department of Health and Human Services, 1982.

West, Victor J. "Federal Land Grants to the States, with Special Reference to Minnesota. Matthias Nordberg Orfield." *Journal of Political Economy* 24, no. 7 (1916): 731–32.

INDEX

ACKNOWLEDGMENTS

I wouldn't be the genealogist I am today if it weren't for the Old Ninety-Six District of South Carolina. This overlooked historic region of South Carolina put me through my research paces. It threw every kind of genealogical hurdle and problem in my direction: complex blended families, multiple family members with the same name, changing surnames, changing ethnic identities, multiethnic families, poorly documented individuals, extreme county boundary changes, generations of cousin marriages, incorrectly identified fathers, and names scrubbed from community memory—Old Ninety-Six introduced me to these issues and many, many, more.

I have been asked numerous times by family, colleagues, and Genealogy Adventures audiences about writing a genealogy-related book over the past decade or so. It was something I had considered; however, the timing was never convenient. When the invitation arrived from Callisto to write a book, I took that as a sign. Now was the time to share what I have learned from my many years of research.

It's not every day you get an opportunity to do what you love, much less receive an invitation to share what you know. I have valued this opportunity. With that in mind, I am so pleased to give you an introductory overview of how to plan and execute your genealogical research in 50 practical steps.

I hope this book inspires you. I hope it supports your quest to discover the stories behind your ancestors becoming Americans—and the experiences they faced in their various life journeys.

ABOUT THE AUTHOR

An engaging and thought-provoking public speaker, Brian Sheffey has expertise in mid-Atlantic and Southern American genealogical research, with an emphasis on the intersection of white, black, and Native American genealogy. He has used his knowledge to solve cases of unknown parentage from colonial America to the present day utilizing DNA and paper trail evidence.

Brian has deep family roots in colonial Virginia and the Carolinas; the Powhatan, Choctaw, and Creek tribes; and the colonial Quaker guarantees in the mid-Atlantic region. His passion for genealogy was inspired by his father's drive and desire to discover the story of his family. This understanding inspires his work to help others uncover their own ancestral stories. He combines over twenty years of experience in marketing research, the entertainment industry, and academia with a passion for genealogical research and a unique ability to solve seemingly impossible cases. His primary research interests include cases of unknown parentage, such as identifying the white progenitors of mulatto family lines, and triangulating answers to tough genealogical questions using traditional records and genetic evidence.

Behind his passion for research lies the belief that genealogy is an opportunity to enable Americans from different backgrounds to connect with each other and make connections around the globe.

Printed in the USA
CPSIA information can be obtained
at www.ICGtesting.com
CBHW042355010524
7764CB00010B/148

9 781646 115662